Volume 18, Number 3, 2017

Quarterly Review
OF Distance
Education

RESEARCH THAT GUIDES PRACTICE

Editors:
Michael Simonson
Charles Schlosser

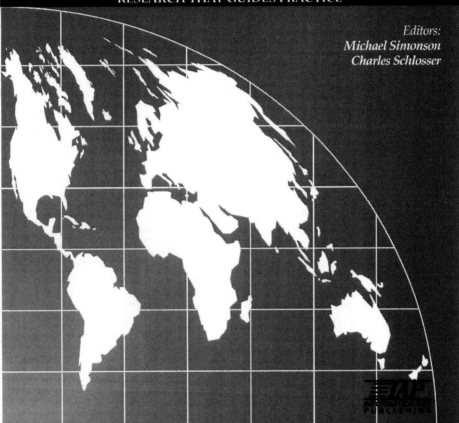

An Official Journal of the
Association for Educational Communications and Technology

Quarterly Review of Distance Education
"Research That Guides Practice"
Volume 18, Number 3, 2017

ARTICLES

STATEMENT OF PURPOSE

The *Quarterly Review of Distance Education* is a rigorously refereed journal publishing articles, research briefs, reviews, and editorials dealing with the theories, research, and practices of distance education. The *Quarterly Review* publishes articles that utilize various methodologies that permit generalizable results which help guide the practice of the field of distance education in the public and private sectors. The *Quarterly Review* publishes full-length manuscripts as well as research briefs, editorials, reviews of programs and scholarly works, and columns. The *Quarterly Review* defines distance education as institutionally based, formal education, where the learning group is separated and where interactive technologies are used to unite the learning group.

DIRECTIONS TO CONTRIBUTORS

Submit four copies of your manuscript, typed double-spaced on 8½ × 11 paper. Manuscripts should be between 10 and 30 pages in length and must conform to the style of the *Publication Manual of the American Psychological Association* (6th ed.). Research Briefs may be shorter, normally between 3 and 10 pages.

The name(s), affiliation(s), address(es), phone numbers, e-mail address(es), and a brief biography of the author(s) should appear on a separate cover page. To ensure anonymity in the review process, names of author(s) should not appear elsewhere in the manuscript, except in appropriate citations. An abstract of 100 words should also be submitted and typed on a separate page.

Printed documents should also be submitted on a flash drive using a recent version of Microsoft Word. The drive should be clearly labeled with the author(s) name(s) and name and version of the word processing program used. Also include an RTF version of the document. Graphics should be in a separate file, clearly labeled, not included as part of the Word document.

Manuscripts will be reviewed by at least three consulting editors. This process normally takes from 3-4 months.

Submit manuscripts to:

Michael Simonson
Charles Schlosser
Editors
Fischler College of Education
Nova Southeastern University
3301 College Avenue
Fort Lauderdale, FL 33314
simsmich@nova.edu

Name of Publication: *Quarterly Review of Distance Education*
(ISSN: 1528-3518)
Issue: Volume 18, Number 3, 2017
Frequency: Quarterly

Office of Publication: IAP–Information Age Publishing, Inc.
P.O. Box 79049
Charlotte, NC 28271-7047
Tel: 704-752-9125
Fax: 704-752-9113
E-mail: QRDE@infoagepub.com
Web Address: www.infoagepub.com

Subscription Rates:

Institutions Print: $200.00
Personal Print: $95.00
Student Print: $65.00

Single Issue Price (print only): Institutions: $45.00, Personal $25.00
Back Issue Special Price (print only): Institutions $100.00;
Personal: $50.00; Student: $35.00
Outside the U.S. please add $25.00 for surface mail.

Editorial Office: *Quarterly Review of Distance Education*
Department of Higher Education Leadership
and Instructional Technology
Fischler College of Education
Nova Southeastern University
3301 College Avenue
Fort Lauderdale, FL 33314
800-986-3223 ext. 8563
simsmich@nova.edu

Quarterly Review of Distance Education is indexed
by the DE Hub Database of Distance Education.

INNOVATIONS IN ACADEMIC SUPPORT
Factors Influencing Student Adoption
of Synchronous Videoconferencing
for Online Support in High-Risk STEM Courses

Donna Rennar-Potacco
William Paterson University

Anymir Orellana
Nova Southeastern University

Andres Salazar
William Paterson University

INTRODUCTION

The low retention rates of students in science, technology, engineering, and mathematics (STEM) and STEM-related majors threaten the ability of the United States to maintain its prominence in science and technology and meet economic demand (Executive Office of the President, President's Council of Advisors on Science and Technology, 2012). Low retention rates also have the potential to influence institutional funding (Gonzalez, 2012; U.S. Senate Committee on Health, Education, Labor & Pensions, 2012) and accreditation (Council of Regional Accrediting Commissions, 2009; Middle States Commission on Higher Education, 2011; U.S. Department of Education, Office of Postsecondary Education, 2008; Wilson, 2012). Reasons provided for these low retention rates include student unpreparedness (Executive Office of the Presi-

dent, President's Council of Advisors on Science and Technology 2012; U.S. Department of Education, National Center for Educational Statistics, 2011), changing student demographics (Consortium for Student Retention Data Exchange Center for Institutional Data Exchange, 2012; National Science Board, 2012; Tossi, 2012; U.S. Department of Education, National Center for Educational Statistics, 2011), and the need to find innovative uses of information technology that enable interactive real-time feedback and decrease educational costs (Executive Office of the President, President's Council of Advisors on Science and Technology, 2012).

Online tutoring through synchronous videoconferencing provides institutions with an alternative form of academic support for students with divergent needs that is effective and interactive. Research in the area of academic support for students at a distance, however,

• **Donna Rennar-Potacco**, Science Enrichment Center, College of Science & Health, William Paterson University, 300 Pompton Road, Wayne, NJ 07470. Telephone: (973) 720-3418. E-mail: PotaccoD@wpunj.edu

The Quarterly Review of Distance Education, Volume 18(3), 2017, pp. 1–17
Copyright © 2017 Information Age Publishing, Inc.
ISSN 1528-3518

remains a relatively underresearched area in this rapidly developing field (Jopling, 2009, 2012; Martinovic, 2009; Shelley, White, Baumann, & Murphy, 2006). Particularly lacking is the identification of factors that influence students to adopt online academic support through synchronous videoconferencing (Dammers, 2009). Since student participation in academic support is typically voluntary, this information can help institution develop online academic support programs more likely to be adopted by its students.

This article presents findings of a qualitative study conducted to understand influences that affected students adoption of an online academic support program delivered through videoconferencing. Theory-driven directed content analysis framed with the diffusion of innovations theory was used to answer the main research question: What are the factors that influence student adoption of online academic support through videoconferencing?

THEORETICAL FRAMEWORK: THE DIFFUSION OF INNOVATIONS

Rogers's (2003) diffusion of innovations theory and Wejnert's (2002) conceptual framework of the diffusion of innovations theory were the theoretical frameworks used to identify adoption influences. According to Rogers, "Diffusion is the process in which an innovation is communicated through certain channels over time among the members of a social system" (p. 5). During this process, when an idea/innovation is introduced and/or invented, it will diffuse and then be adopted or rejected. The extent, rate, outcomes, and consequences of this diffusion can vary according to environmental conditions, the characteristics of the decision making unit, and the characteristics of the innovation (Rogers, 2003; Simonson, 2012). Wejnert (2002) expanded on Rogers's theory, proposing a framework that conceptualized, integrated, and grouped diffusion variables into three concepts: (a) the environmental context, (b) the characteristics

of innovations, and (c) the characteristics of innovators that will influence an individual's probability of adopting the innovation.

The Influences of Environmental Context

The first component in Wejnert's (2002) framework describes characteristics of the environmental context that "modulate diffusion via structural characteristics of the modern world[–]geographical settings, societal culture, political conditions, and global uniformity" (p. 297), that can influence an innovator's adoption of an innovation. These influences may be related to trends, economics, funding, barriers, and demand. These influences may also be interwoven with characteristics of the innovation and innovator, such as available resources, previous experience, perceived needs and/or problems, degree of innovativeness, and accepted norms (Rogers, 2003; Simonson, 2012).

Innovation-Based Influences

The second component in Wejnert's (2002) conceptual framework is characteristics of the innovation that can influence an individual's decision to adopt an innovation, such as perceived benefits versus costs and consequences. Rogers (2003) identified five attributes that influence these characteristics: relative advantage, compatibility, complexity, trialability, and observability.

Relative advantage, which is the ratio of expected benefits to the costs of the innovation's adoption (Rogers, 2003), can be influenced by characteristics that are important to users, such as economic profitability, low cost, convenience, decrease in discomfort, social prestige, savings in time and effort, and incentives. An additional factor influencing adoption is the compatibility of the decision-making unit's, or innovator's, values, experiences, and needs with the complexity, trialability, and the observability of the innovation (Rogers, 2003; Wejnert, 2002). That is, the more difficult it is for individuals to find a product, understand what it does, and/or use it, the less likely they are to adopt. In contrast, "The easier it is for individuals to see [observe] the results of an innovation, the more likely they are to adopt" (Rogers, 2003, p. 17).

Innovator-Related Influences

The last component of Wejnert's (2002) conceptual framework is the characteristics of innovators that influence their perceptions of the costs and benefits of adopting the innovation. The susceptibility of individuals to these influences may be related to the potential adopter's demographic status, familiarity with the innovation, and/or socioeconomic status (Wejnert, 2002). Marketing strategies, change agents, and social networks are some of the influences that have been effective in motivating target markets to investigate an innovation (Rogers, 2003).

METHODOLOGY

Two forms of qualitative data were used to develop a more complete understanding of factors that influenced student adoption of online academic support through videoconferencing: participant observation of all groups and processes during the semester, and a semistructured interview of students and academic tutors at the end of the semester.

Participants and Setting

The site of the investigation was an academic support center that services students enrolled in courses offered by the College of Science and Health. This college is located within a 4-year public Hispanic-serving university in the Northeast serving approximately 11,500 students (William Paterson University, 2015).

Student participants were selected using purposeful, nonprobability sampling of all students enrolled in a science or statistics course at the university during the Spring of 2014 who received a minimum of 1–1.5 hours of online academic support. Twenty-one students satisfied these criteria and participated in the study. Twenty of these participants finished the program and gave interviews. The average age of these online students (25) was significantly greater than students who used face-to-face tutoring (22). There was no significant difference between the average GPA of students who came for tutoring online (2.85), compared to students who chose face-to-face (2.96) tutoring (Potacco, 2015; Potacco, Orellana, Chen, & Salazar, 2016). Tutor participants were selected using purposeful, nonprobability sampling of all tutors who tutored at least one student 1 or more hours online through the online tutoring program, had previous experience tutoring students in high-risk science courses face-to-face at the academic support center, and had a GPA greater than 3.0. Five tutors fulfilled these requirements and participated in the study.

Data Collection Procedures

The researcher visited high-risk science courses during the first 2 weeks of the spring semester in order to recruit student participants. Tutors were recruited at the beginning of the semester by an individual at the center who had no authority over them. Thereafter, participants were asked to attend an orientation in the use of the online tutoring platform, Blackboard Collaborate (BBC), using the computer and equipment they intended to use for their online sessions. The majority of orientations were given onsite at the center. Students unable to attend face-to-face orientations were provided with a synchronous online orientation using BBC. Tutor orientations, which were more comprehensive, were all face-to-face. After the orientation, the researcher scheduled an online academic support session for each student with a trained tutor proficient in the subject. The types of STEM courses tutored online were in the disciplines of chemistry, mathematics, biology, physics, anatomy, and physiology. Whenever possible, applicants were scheduled to join an existing online study group, provided the course and their schedules were compatible.

Participant observation was used to study participant activities and interactions with the program and each other in the physical and technological environment (Creswell, 2013) and to gain the trust of other participants (Glesne, 2011). An unstructured observational protocol was used to capture a holistic perspective of the setting (Zacharias, 2012) and detect unanticipated, but important, phenomena and themes of interest (American Association for the Advancement of Science, 2012; McKechnie, 2008). An observational journal was used to record events, social interactions, activities, insights, and reflective field notes (Creswell, 2013; Glesne, 2011).

Within 2 weeks of the student's termination of online academic support, a one-on-one semistructured interview of approximately 1 hour was scheduled with each student in order to provide participants with an opportunity to reveal alternative perspectives and/or perceptions and acquire information that was not observed (Glesne, 2011). Most interviews were held face-to-face. It was necessary, however, to interview several student participants synchronously through BBC due to their inability to meet face-to-face. All interviews were in the presence of a peer observer who took notes from an unobtrusive area in the office or online.

An interview protocol was followed in order to increase reliability by providing a constant structure that guided the research and reduced the potential of data collection inconsistencies between interviewees. The interview questions and protocol were developed and refined through a pilot test of respondents representative of the target populations (Creswell, 2013). Students and tutors were given participant-specific preambles and interview questions.

At the end of the interview, the researcher used member-checking to go over the response notes with the participant and peer observer to verify the accuracy of these notes (Creswell,

2013). Student participants who completed at least one academic support session and the interview were compensated at the rate of $3.00 per tutoring session and $15.00 for the interview. Students receiving online academic support also received documentation of tutoring attendance through a coupon point that could be exchanged for credit in some courses. Consistent with the center's coupon program, this incentive was also provided to face-to-face students. Tutors were compensated per their normal salary structure.

Data Analysis

Data generated from observation and the interviews were analyzed using theory-driven directed content analysis. This form of analysis uses a deductive strategy in which the initial coding scheme is developed before data analysis, based on theory or relevant research, and refined during the analysis (Elo & Kyngäs, 2008; Gläser & Laudel, 2013). Following is a description of the four stages of this data analysis:

Stage 1. The data were deidentified with a number coding scheme, then extracted to one or more of the categories and subcategories of the initial coding scheme by question and participant group using a code-recode procedure in order to augment coding reliability.

Stage 2. A final coding scheme was created by modifying, eliminating, and/or renaming categories and subcategories to more accurately describe responses in the data. Coding validity of this final scheme was augmented through the use of low-inference descriptors, such as direct quotations to validate themes, and triangulation (Kimberlin & Winterstein, 2008).

Stage 3. Inductive analysis was used to identify themes within and across the participant groups that emerged from the deductively derived categories and subcategories. Thereafter, these data were reduced with the intention of retaining each respondent's perspective, while striving for clarification, understanding, and explanation. These nine themes and exam-

TABLE 1
Adoption Influences

Inductive Themes	Relationship	Example
Pedagogy	Online teaching methods and instruction	"The tools ... actually worked pretty effectively in answering my questions and teaching the material."
Interaction	Communication dynamics, and/or transactional distance factors	"[The program] made it easier for me to e-mail questions to the tutors and ask about it the next session."
Technology	Characteristics of the online platform.	"I didn't like how long the images took to load."
Technical support	Online technical support factors	"Once I came into the center and the coordinator showed me how to use it on my phone ... my confidence was restored."
Convenience	Influences related to time, effort, scheduling, commuting, etc.	"My tutor was also available by e-mail and text if we had a problem."
Logistics	The operation and management of the program	"There were too many people on too many levels ... if there were three academically close students in the same session, I would have benefited more."
Demographics	Characteristics of adopters that emerged within and across categories and subcategories.	"I used Skype in the past ... well, my generation ... because I am always on my computer doing e-mail and homework. I figured I should use that."
Reward	Extrinsic and intrinsic incentives	"The tutoring session allowed me to always get the As no matter where I was."
The future	Adopters' perception of the impact of adoption on their future.	"Videoconferencing will be regularly used in education, business, and our personal lives in the future."

ples of text coded to these themes are provided in Table 1

Stage 4. All results were integrated through a triangulation of the data in order to compare and contrast findings; identify patterns, issues, corroborations and discrepancies of perspective between the participant groups; reveal gaps in the research that merited further investigation; derive a more comprehensive understanding of the findings; and increase the validity and reliability of the data.

RESULTS AND DISCUSSION

A complex interaction of factors related to the environmental context of the adoption, the characteristics of the innovation, and the characteristics of the innovator influenced students' adoption of online academic support through videoconferencing. It was also evident that, within each category, there were subcategories with the potential to enable or impede

adoption in a complex, interactive process that involved various stakeholders. Figure 1 provides an overview of this interaction of adoption influences.

Environmental Context

Issues related to the environmental context that influenced student adoption of the innovation encompassed marketing, training, the platform, technical support, culture, attitudes, trends, and connectedness.

Marketing. The marketing strategies that were most effective in motivating students to investigate the program were classroom visitation and referral by professors and classmates. Extra credit points provided through the center's coupon program were also identified by all participants as a primary motive for student adoption of the online program. This finding is consistent with previous studies (Potacco & De Young, 2007; Potacco, Chen,

Adoption influences

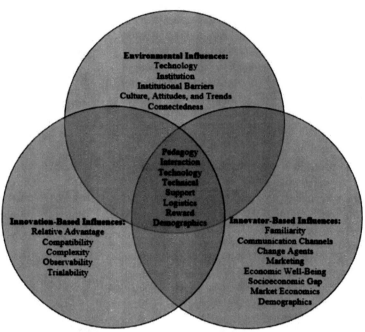

FIGURE 1
Interaction of Factors Influencing Students' Adoption
of Online Academic Support Through Videoconferencing

Desroches, Chisholm, & De Young, 2013) that have demonstrated the ability of the coupon incentive program to motivate students to seek academic support face-to-face. The practice of using incentives to increase academic performance and task interest has also been documented by others (Ash, 2008; Brewer & Klein, 2006; Haywood, Kuespert, Madecky, & Nor, 2008). In addition to the extra credit, many adopters were influenced by innovation-centered incentives, such as the ability to "get help," improve their grades, convenience, and/ or the ability to "save money."

Training. The orientation appeared to influence continued adoption, since students who had an orientation attended a significantly greater number of sessions on average, than students who did not attend an orientation (Potacco, 2015). The tutee orientation provided the staff with the opportunity to develop

a relationship with the tutee and discuss the roles and responsibilities of the tutor, tutee, and technical support. The orientation also provided students with a more realistic image of the online experience in agreement with Bozarth, Chapman, and LaMonica (2004).

Students valued learning how to log into the room, set up audio, switch between screens, copy and paste pictures, text in the chat box, and use drawing tools to write on the whiteboard. Tutors valued learning how to use the online platform and develop the pedagogical skills needed to communicate effectively in the online environment, as described by Richardson (2009) and Stickler and Hampel (2007).

The Platform. Gunawardena and Duphorne (2000) suggested that the features of an online platform are one of the best predictors of learner satisfaction. Participants in this study commented that the online platform was "easily accessible ... easy to download" and appreciated the ability to log into the program from various locations and devices. The mobile phone became a dependable default that could be used when audio issues arose or students could not access a computer. The increasing use of mobile devices by students has also been reported by Dahlstrom (2012, 2013); Johnson, Adams, and Cummins (2012); and Johnson, Adams Becker, Cummins, Estrada, Freeman, and Ludgate (2013).

Relative to utility, participants indicated that the platform was effective in presenting content, providing feedback, and facilitating learning. Users in this study were particularly impressed with the wide range of tools available in the platform. The activities that were most valued included drawing and solving problems on the whiteboard, and the ability to work together using audio and visual features. The importance of the audio and visual characteristics of the medium for the adoption and use of technology in distance education was also emphasized by Gunawardena and McIsaac (2004).

In contrast, technological issues resulted in participant frustration and acted as barriers to adoption, in agreement with previous studies (Liu, Gomez, Khan, & Yen, 2007; McBrien, Cheng & Jones, 2009; Shea, Pickett, & Li, 2005). The most common technical issues encountered were delays in audio, room, and content loading; the inability to launch the room; and connection and audio issues. Microphone problems and difficulties signing onto sessions have also been reported by others (Little, Passmore, & Schullo, 2006; McBrien et al., 2009).

Technical Support. Researchers have reported the importance of reliable technical support and training in influencing an online learners' ability to achieve successful outcomes (e.g., Jopling, 2012; Liu et al., 2007 [Citation not listed in references; McBrien et al., 2009; Rice, 2006; Selvi, 2010; Simonson, Schlosser, & Orellana, 2011; Tallent-Runnels, Cooper, Lan, Thomas, & Busby, 2005, Tallent-Runnels et al., 2006). Thus, a substantial

effort was made to provide expedient, efficacious support to program participants that included orientations, tutor mentoring in online pedagogy, and technical support before and during sessions. Subsequently, tutees commented that support positively impacted their confidence by "clearing up any questions," showing them "what to do to be able to communicate," and explaining "how to use the applications." Tutors commented that the orientation, staff feedback, and other online tutors helped them gain confidence and support students' efforts to log in, use the program, and negotiate technical issues. These findings are consistent with Tallent-Runnels et al.'s (2005) observation that, with support, instructors could also learn how to help students with minor technical problems.

Culture, Attitudes, Trends, and Connectedness. Two environmentally based perceptions influenced participant adoption from a broader societal or global perspective. One perception was that most people in their age group had a "good general knowledge" of online applications and regularly communicated with others through videoconferencing. The second perception was that students needed to be able to communicate with others through videoconferencing for education and business. Students' perception that technology had the ability to help them achieve their academic goals and prepare for future academic and workplace activities was also reported by an ECAR survey of 113,035 students (Dahlstrom, 2013).

Program adoption was also motivated by connectedness in that many tutees reported that they began the program as a result of referral by a classmate, professor, or center staff member. Continued program adoption was motivated by the development of relationships between the tutee with other tutees and the tutor within their online learning community.

Innovation-Based Influences

Characteristics of the innovation that influenced adopters included the relative advantages and consequences of adopting the innovation, and the compatibility, complexity, and perceptions perceived by the student through observation and/or trial.

Relative Advantage. The relative advantage of online tutoring perceived by participants was influenced by demographics and demands related to work, family, physical disability, scheduling, and/or travel. As an example, one tutee reluctantly began online tutoring because she was in academic jeopardy, but could not attend tutoring face-to-face because of a 3-hour commute and the need to stay home with her children. Although this student expressed reluctance to use the technology, she adopted online tutoring because it provided a relative advantage, compared to the consequence of not being able to get academic support.

Relative advantage can also be perceived by distance learners through the reduction of transactional distance enabled by synchronous videoconferencing. McBrien et al. (2009) suggested that transactional distance is a complex phenomenon, however, influenced by numerous overlapping elements that should be studied holistically, along with factors related to interaction. Interactions affecting the adoption of online tutoring are discussed in the three categories described by Moore (2007, 2013): learner-learner, learner-media, and learner-instructor.

Learner-Learner. Social presence and the extent to which the technology enables the learner to interact with other learners and instructors has been identified as important to the adoption and use of a technology at a distance (Gunawardena & McIsaac, 2004). In agreement, tutors engendered social presence by uploading amusing welcome screens, using their cameras, texting emoticons, responding to tutees by name, maintaining a positive atmosphere, and motivating group work. The practice of creating a welcoming online environment using these strategies has also been recommended by others (Hastie, Chen, & Kuo, 2007; Little et al., 2006; Packham, Jones, Thomas, & Miller, 2006).

The use of cameras also helped to create a more personable environment. Gunawardena and McIsaac (2004) suggested this action contributes to the level of intimacy of the communications medium. Hastie et al. (2007) discussed the ability of the webcam to help online students, who may not have the same opportunities as face-to-face students, interact and develop a community with their peers. Webcams also served the purpose of providing tutors with paralinguistic cues. One tutor noted, "Since there was no visual of their [the tutees'] face, it was hard to tell if they really understood ... one had to constantly ask if they understood or not." Another tutor remarked that "it was like I was talking to the whiteboard. I think it definitely makes a difference because there is that interaction that you are actually talking to someone." Consistent with these findings, previous studies have recognized the challenge of communicating with students online without seeing facial expressions or paralinguistic cues (Chen, Liao, Chen, & Lee, 2011; Kersaint, Dogbey, Barber, & Kephart, 2011; McBrien et al., 2009; Ng, 2007).

The need for webcams was also influenced by group size. Tutees in larger groups that did not use cameras complained that tutees talked over one another and commented that it was difficult to determine "who knew what" and "who was doing what." Consequently, tutors did not know who was confused, participating, asking questions, and/or in need of attention. Group size also affected interaction. Although participants appreciated the opportunity to share, explain, and discuss information learned with peers through group work, as discussed by Hunt, Eagle, and Kitchen (2004) and Ozkan (2010), participants commented that the smaller groups were more personal. As one tutor commented, "If you are in a smaller group, you have more interaction with a tutee."

Students had mixed opinions concerning the use of webcams. Some students missed seeing body language during sessions when tutees did not use cameras; other students indicated they felt more comfortable asking questions without other people looking at them. The ability for synchronous online platforms to allow shy students to feel more comfortable expressing their opinions was also discussed by McBrien et al. (2009).

Learner-Media. The argument that media is a vehicle that delivers content and that learning gains result from instructional design theory and practice began with Clark (1994, 2001) and has continued to be discussed rigorously by others (Holden & Westfall, 2010; Simonson et al., 2011). Bernard et al. (2004) described technology as a tool that enables collaborative and complex learning if appropriate activities and strategies are employed through guided, interactive communication. Aragon, Johnson, and Shaik (2002), suggested novel, engaging, and entertaining activities appeal to learners with different learning styles and preferences. Sorensen and Baylen (2009) found that active learning tools, such as animations, graphing, problem-based learning, and games, increased student participation and engaged students with diverse learning needs. Isaksen and Ramberg (2005) discussed using cases, games, simulation, chat, and other involvement activities, as well as frequent and immediate feedback, to increase interactivity.

Participants drew, chatted, took snapshots, used digital resources, and/or shared software applications to interact with each other. Media-enabled interactivity most valued included watching videos, taking practice tests, interacting with diagrams and slides, sharing online graphics, and discussing concepts with each other through the chat box. Two activities particularly appreciated by this STEM population were the abilities to work together on scientific and mathematical problems using the whiteboard and external technology programs using application sharing.

Technology-related variables related to the media can also affect interaction. Holden and Westfall (2010) cited the importance of portability, visual clarity, the ability to update content quickly, and bandwidth in the utility of technology. In agreement, interaction was supported by high quality audio and visual effects.

Participants appreciated that communicating with the online platform was "like talking face-to-face" and "the same as sitting in front of someone with my notes and books open." In contrast, interaction was negatively affected by content and audio delays, resulting from bandwidth issues. Students also needed to be able to access the media portably from laptops and through smartphones.

Learner-Instructor Interaction. Gunawardena and McIsaac (2004) suggested that students can be motivated through learner-instructor dialogue and feedback that facilitates learning and reduces transactional distance. Macintyre and Macdonald (2011) found that students' connection to their tutor could mediate perceptions of remoteness. In agreement, tutees commented that their online experience "inspired" them to "stay in the room after the session to work together," and/or "study more … to be better prepared to interact in online tutoring session activities."

A multimodal learning environment and alternative teaching techniques, strategies, and equipment can also be utilized to enhance interactivity (Aragon et al., 2002; Johnson & Aragon, 2003; McBrien et al., 2009; Moreno & Mayer, 2007). Concomitantly, tutees commented on the diversity and effectiveness of techniques and tools used by their tutors during sessions. The instructional strategies most commonly lauded by tutees were "taking content and breaking it down into something I could understand," "explaining it [concepts] in a different way," "using anecdotes and life situations," "feedback," "application sharing," "group problem-solving on the whiteboard," and interacting with "practice tests, games, and videos."

Consequences. Consistent with Hadfield, Jopling, Royle, and Southern's (2009) suggestion that the adoption of a technology is related to its perceived utility and applicability to the adopter, the predominant consequences that influenced adoption were convenience, interaction, extrinsic reward, and the technology.

The convenience of being able to find help anywhere, anytime was an important positive consequence of online tutoring, consistent with previous findings (e.g., Gunawardena & McIsaac, 2004; Little et al., 2006; Means, Toyama, Murphy, Bakia, & Jones, 2010; Ng, 2007; Rice, 2006; Smith, Salaway, & Caruso, 2009; Stanford-Bowers, 2008; Tallent-Runnels et al., 2006; Wilson, 2012). In general, students expressed the inability to attend face-to-face sessions due to work, physical disability, family responsibilities, schedule conflicts, and/or other challenges, such as commuting. Numerous students commented that the flexibility of online tutoring enabled them to avoid traffic, distance, and time on the road. As one tutee commented, "What really influenced me to do this program was my commuting status. I live far away." Another tutor noted,

> It was hard getting to school this winter with all the potholes and snow apocalypse. I feel a little nervous taking my car places when I don't have to … all the stress involved in commuting and getting gas. I could just focus on what I needed to do.

Another tutee who needed to use his phone and online tutoring due to his work schedule and a long commute commented, "The tutoring session allowed me to always get the As no matter where I was … whether I was in the car in south Jersey or north Jersey."

Positive academic and social consequences were also attributed to online tutoring. Academically, students acknowledged that online tutoring "helped me stay on a routine," "motivated me to keep studying," and "helped me to improve my grades." Socially, students revealed that online tutoring provided them with the ability to interact with their peers online "just like in person" and "feed off of other classmates." Tutors agreed that tutees benefited through their ability to work with other students in groups. Rewards, such as bonus points, grade improvement, more effective studying habits, and videoconferencing expertise were other positive consequences discussed by participants. Perceived tutor benefits included "helped me reinforce content previously learned," "was a great opportunity

to have a different method to tutor," "increased my confidence to communicate online," and "can be used in my education, profession, and personal life."

Compatibility. Compatibility of the program with the needs and wants of a potential adopter can promote adoption (Rogers, 2003). Accordingly, the availability of academic help was compatible with the needs of students unable to obtain face-to-face academic support due to work, family, commuting, physical disability, and other challenges. Additionally, the efficacy of the platform was compatible with students' need for an effective medium that could be used to learn collaboratively, access online resources, and improve academic outcomes (Potacco, 2015).

Observability, Trialability, and Complexity. There is a multifaceted relationship between the observability, trialability, and complexity of an innovation and its familiarity to the innovator. That is, complexity has the potential to be a barrier to adoption, but it can be reduced through familiarity with the innovation resulting from observation and trial. Furthermore, if the trial or observation is perceived as a positive consequence and familiar to the student, adoption is more likely. In accord with this rationale, most participants indicated that their decision to adopt the innovation was based on other videoconferencing programs previously observed, used, and valued.

Based on participants' comments that the program was easy to download and use, the complexity of the platform was not an issue. However, since more students continued adoption of the program when an orientation and technical support was provided, the orientation may have influenced these perceptions. This suggestion was corroborated by tutees who expressed increased confidence as a result of "hands on" instruction and receiving guidance from the staff during their orientation and tutoring sessions, and tutors who expressed confidence with the platform and online pedagogy as a result of practice and mentoring. This suggestion is also consistent with Shea et al.'s (2005) finding that technical and human support can help online instructors overcome complexity issues that can impede technology adoption.

Innovator-Related Influences

Innovator-related factors that influenced adoption included communication channels, change agents, pedagogy, and socioeconomics.

Communication Channels and Change Agents. The program's most successful marketing efforts were made through peers, tutors, the program administrator, and professors. Peers in social networks persuaded classmates to join their sessions. Tutors acted as change agents by providing their tutees with "guidance," "feedback," and support, through their roles as mentor, role model, and coach. The program administrator acted as a change agent by directing the attention of students and professors to the program, providing them with information about the program(s), and supplying technical support to participants. Professors acted as change agents by motivating their students to seek academic support through referral and the coupon incentive program. As one student remarked, it was "definitely the coupon points because my professor gave us the opportunity to gain points toward the exams."

Pedagogy. Tutees acknowledged that tutors motivated them to continue their adoption of online tutoring through tutoring strategies and activities used during sessions and the effect these strategies had on their academic outcomes. All tutors participated in an orientation; however, pedagogical expertise developed experientially. As recognized by Bernard et al. (2004) and Wang (2005), most of our instructors were unaware of the unique pedagogy of online education and continued traditional face-to-face practices during initial tutoring sessions. With practice, however, the pedagogical proficiency of the tutors improved. As noted by one tutee, the tutor "grew with us and her teaching style got better as we had more sessions." Concomitantly, tutors acknowledged that student and staff feedback helped them integrate face-to-face and online approaches and gain confidence using the online pedagogy

Socioeconomic Characteristics. Socioeconomic characteristics influencing adoption included demographics, market economics, economic well-being, and the socioeconomic gap.

Demographics. There was no significant difference in gender, class standing, commuter status, or ethnicity between students who chose online tutoring versus face-to-face tutoring. There were significant differences, however, in the proportion of commuters and age of students who chose online tutoring versus face-to-face tutoring (Potacco, 2015; Potacco et al., 2016). This finding is in agreement with Radford (2011) who described online learners as undergraduate students who are older, have dependents, a spouse, full-time employment, and/or mobile disabilities and Chen, Gonyea, and Kuh (2008) who cite the demand for distance learning by commuters. As noted by one tutee, "I have two part-time jobs that require me to work 40 to 50 hours per week and I am a full-time student … it takes me 1 hour and 30 minutes to get from my home to school."

Another student, restricted to a wheelchair and with a limited ability to write, stated:

> Online tutoring provided solutions to some physical problems that I had due to my muscle disease. It was difficult to hold the phone up and sometimes difficult to write.... If I had a tutor in person, there would be more writing for me and that would be difficult because my hands get tired. In this way, I just have to type.

Technology experience also influenced adoption, based on the large proportion of participants (91%) declaring previous experience with videoconferencing and other technologies. Concomitantly, almost all participants demonstrated the ability to learn the program quickly, suggesting familiarity and confidence with the technology used in this program. The positive relationship of previous computer experience with online use has also been recognized by others (Holcomb, King, & Brown, 2004; Hunt et al., 2004; Smith et al., 2009; Tallent-Runnels et al., 2006).

Market Economics. Market economics influenced participants attempting to position themselves more strategically in their profession. Students revealed that their STEM courses were required for a profession in health care, and that their entry into these programs required competitive grades and time-intensive volunteer activities in medically oriented endeavors. Online tutoring was perceived as a means to acquire the academic help needed to reach these goals while fulfilling their family and/or work responsibilities. As one student commented, "I hoped it would help me get to my ultimate goal, which is to go to medical school … so I would hope it would help me get a good grade." This finding is consistent with Tallent-Runnels et al.'s (2006) suggestion that online students were older, highly motivated, and focused on achieving specific learning outcomes. From another perspective, many tutors and students also believed it was "important to be comfortable with videoconferencing and technology" and discussed the future economic benefits of learning a technological skill that had the potential to help them "in their future education, career, and personal lives."

Economic Well-Being. Most tutees stressed that the program enabled them to get the help they needed while they continued to maintain the economic well-being of themselves and their families. For this reason, most tutees needed to schedule their sessions late at night, 8:00 p.m. or 9:00 p.m., after their children were put to bed or they finished working. Additionally, online participants cited the ability to avoid costly travel expenses.

Socioeconomic Gap. The majority of tutees reported fewer opportunities to access face-to-face academic support due to their family responsibilities, demanding work schedules, transportation challenges, and/or conflicts in course schedules. Another subset of tutees had no access to technology or inferior broadband capacity, as previously discussed by Wenger White, Smith, and Rowe (2005). These conditions can precipitate a socioeconomic gap that results in disparities between the academic outcomes and retention of students who can and cannot find academic support compatible with their needs. Consistent with this finding, Tinto (2006) stated that students from low income families have fewer opportunities to attend college full time, not work, and attain their bachelor's degree within 6 years. Online tutoring with this mobile platform helped bridge this socioeconomic gap by providing these students with an equal opportunity to receive efficacious academic support.

LIMITATIONS

The results reported by this study were derived in a real-world environment where variables could be observed naturally and threats related to novelty effects, characteristics of the stimulus and settings, and experimental conditions are minimized to increase external validity (Gravetter & Forzano, 2011). In an effort to minimize negative internal validity effects, environmental and program variables were kept consistent, and multiple methods and sources were used to enhance the validity, reliability, and trustworthiness of these findings, including member checking, code recoding, and the triangulation of the findings. Since participants in this study were exclusively involved with science and statistics courses at one higher education institution, results may vary across groups in other disciplines and in other higher education institutions differing in structure, setting, and geographical location. Furthermore, since practical and ethical considerations prohibited random assignment of participants, students were self-selected and may have been exposed to both face-to-face and online tutoring. Possible exposure in these cases may have influenced perceptions and/or resulted in more informed responses.

CONCLUSIONS AND RECOMMENDATIONS

A complex interaction of characteristics related to the environmental context of the program, the program, and the student influenced students' adoption of online academic support through videoconferencing.

The Platform. Important considerations in the selection of a platform should include visibility, reliability, user friendliness, and hardware requirements. The platform should also offer a wide range of tools that enable synchronous modes of communication, such as videoconferencing, application sharing, whiteboard, and Internet access.

Demographic Groups. Institutions should strategically target the demographic groups most likely to adopt online tutoring in order to maximize their allocation of resources. Students who adopted online academic support were previous adopters of other technologies who had experience with videoconferencing; commuters; mature; and challenged by family, work, and/or physical disability.

Marketing. A number of marketing techniques were effective in promoting adoption. Recommendation by professors and peers, and the incentive of extra credit points for active participation in academic support were the most productive strategies. Adoption was also influenced by effective academic assistance that students perceived helped them improve their academic outcomes.

Tutors, Training, and Technical Support. Tutors should have good content and technical expertise and be willing to acquire the necessary technological and pedagogical expertise needed to be effectual in the online environment. Institutions providing online tutoring through videoconferencing need to make the commitment to provide training and orientations for program participants. Additionally, technical support should be time sensitive, taught to tutors during the orientation, and available as a service from the institution and/or platform provider.

Pedagogy and Interaction. Tutors should be encouraged to use a wide range of online teaching tools and strategies that is appropriate for the discipline. Tutors should be required and students encouraged to use Webcams. Participants in online groups should be at the same academic level, studying the same academic content, and limited in size.

This program provided students with divergent needs and enrolled in STEM courses with alternative form of academic support that was effective and interactive (Potacco, 2015; Potacco et al., 2016). It also enabled students, who did not have the same opportunities as face-to-face students to interact and develop a community with their peers. This research also identified factors that influenced students to adopt this program. A consideration of these factors can be used by institutions to design, develop, and support an efficacious online tutoring program that is more likely to be adopted by its students.

Acknowledgment: The results of this publication were derived from a more extensive investigation conducted for a doctoral dissertation titled "A Mixed Method Study of the Adoption of Online Academic Support by STEM students in Higher Education" (Potacco, 2015).

REFERENCES

American Association for the Advancement of Science. (2012). Describing & measuring undergraduate STEM teaching practices: A report from a national meeting on the measurement of undergraduate science, technology, engineering and mathematics (STEM) teaching. Retrieved from http://ccliconference.org/files/2013/11/Measuring-STEM-Teaching-Practices.pdf

Aragon, S. R., Johnson, S. D., & Shaik, N. (2002). The influence of learning style preferences on student success in online versus face-to-face environments. *The American Journal of Distance Education, 16,* 227–243. http://dx.doi.org/10.1207/S15389286AJDE1604_3

Ash, K. (2008, February 13). Promises of money meant to heighten student motivation. *Education Week.* Retrieved from http://www.edweek.org

Bernard, R. M., Abrami, P. C., Lou, Y., Borok-hovski, E., Wade, C. A., Wozney, L., ... Huang, B. (2004). How does distance education compare with classroom instruction? A meta-analysis of the empirical literature. *Review of Educational Research, 74,* 379–439. http://dx.doi.org/10.3102/00346543074003379

Bozarth, J., Chapman, D. D., & LaMonica, L. (2004). Preparing for distance learning: Designing an online student orientation course. *Educational Technology & Society, 7*(1), 87–106. Retrieved from http://www.ifets.info/

Brewer, S., & Klein, J. D. (2006). Type of positive interdependence and affiliation motive in an asynchronous, collaborative learning environment. *Association for Educational Communications and Technology, 54,* 331–354. http://dx.doi.org/10.1007/s11423-006-9603-3

Chen, C.-H., Liao, C.-H., Chen, Y.-C., & Lee, C.-F. (2011). The integration of synchronous communication technology into service learning for preservice teachers' online tutoring of middle school students. *The Internet and Higher Education, 14,* 27–33. http://dx.doi.org/10.1016/j.iheduc.2010.02.003

Chen, P.-S. D., Gonyea, R., & Kuh, G. (2008). Learning at a distance: Engaged or not. *Innovate: Journal of Online Education, 4*(3), Art. 5. Retrieved from http://www.editlib.org/j/IJOE/

Clark, R. E. (1994). Media will never influence learning. *Educational Technology Research and Development, 42*(2), 21–29. http://dx.doi.org/10.1007/BF02299088

Clark, R. E. (2001). Media are "mere vehicles": The opening argument. In R. E. Clark (Ed.), *Learning from media: Arguments, analysis, and evidence* (pp. 1–12). Greenwich, CT: Information Age.

Consortium for Student Retention Data Exchange, Center for Institutional Data Exchange (CSRDE). (2012). *The retention and graduation rates of entering baccalaureate degree-seeking freshman cohorts from fall 2001 through fall 2010* [2011–12 CSRDE retention report]. Retrieved from http://csrde.ou.edu/web/reports.html

Council of Regional Accrediting Commissions. (2009). *Guidelines for the evaluation of distance education (on-line learning).* Retrieved from http://www.ncahlc.org/Information-for-Institutions/publications.html

Creswell, J. W. (2013). *Qualitative inquiry and research design: Choosing among five approaches* (4th ed.). Thousand Oaks, CA: SAGE.

Dahlstrom, E. (2012). *ECAR study of undergraduate students and information technology, 2012* [Research report]. Retrieved from http://www.educause.edu

Dahlstrom, E. (2013). *ECAR study of undergraduate students and information technology, 2013* [Research report]. Retrieved from http://www.educause.edu

Dammers, R. J. (2009). Utilizing Internet-based videoconferencing for instrumental music lessons. *Applications of Research in Music Education, 28*(1), 17–24. http://dx.doi.org/10.1177/8755123309344159

Elo, S., & Kyngäs, H. (2008). The qualitative content analysis process. *Journal of Advanced Nursing, 62,* 107–115. http://dx.doi.org/10.1111/j.1365-2648.2007.04569.x

Executive Office of the President, President's Council of Advisors on Science and Technology. (2012, February). Report to the president: Engage to excel: Producing one million additional college graduates with degrees in science, technology, engineering, and mathematics. Retrieved from https://www.whitehouse.gov

Gläser, J., & Laudel, G. (2013). Life with and without coding: Two methods for early-stage data analysis in qualitative research aiming at causal explanations. *Forum: Social Qualitative Research, 14*(2), Art. 5. Retrieved from http://www.qualitative-research.net/index.php/fqs/index

Glesne, C. (2011). *Becoming qualitative researchers: An introduction* (4th ed.). Boston, MA: Pearson.

Gonzalez, A. (2012, August 3). California cuts University of Phoenix off from student aid funds. *Phoenix Business Journal.* Retrieved from http://www.bizjournals.com/phoenix

Gravetter, F. J., & Forzano, L.-A. B. (2011). *Research methods for the behavioral sciences* (4th ed.). Belmont, CA: Wadsworth Cengage.

Gunawardena, C. N., & Duphorne, P. L. (2000). Predictors of learner satisfaction in an academic computer conference. *Distance Education, 21,* 101–117. http://dx.doi.org/10.1080/0158791000210107

Gunawardena, C. N., & McIsaac, M. S. (2004). Distance education. In D. H. Jonassen (Ed.), *Handbook of research for educational communications and technology* (2nd ed., pp. 355–396). Mahwah, NJ: Erlbaum.

Hadfield, M., Jopling, M., Royle, K., & Southern, L. (2009). *Evaluation of the training and development agency for schools' funding for ICT in ITT projects* (Final report). Retrieved from http://www.academia.edu/184568/Evaluation_of_the_Training_and_Development_Agency_for_Schools_funding_for_ICT_in_ITT_Projects

Hastie, M., Chen, N.-S., & Kuo, Y.-H. (2007). Instructional design for best practice in the synchronous cyber classroom. *Journal of Educational Technology and Society, 10*(4), 281–294. Retrieved from http://www.ifets.info/

Haywood, J., Kuespert, S., Madecky, D., & Nor, A. (2008). *Increasing elementary and high school student motivation through the use of extrinsic and intrinsic rewards* (Unpublished master's thesis). Retrieved from ERIC database. (ED503268)

Holcomb, L. B., King, F. B., & Brown, S. W. (2004). Student traits and attributes contributing to success in online courses: Evaluation of university online courses. *Journal of Interactive Online Learning, 2*(3), Art. 4. Retrieved from http://www.ncolr.org

Holden, J. T., & Westfall, P. J.-L. (with Gamor, K. I.). (2010). *An instructional media selection guide for distance learning-Implications for blended learning—Implications for blended learning featuring an introduction to virtual worlds* (2nd ed.). Retrieved from http://www.usdla.org/v/assets/pdf_files/AIMSGDL2ndEd._styled_010311.pdf

Hunt, L., Eagle, L., & Kitchen, P. J. (2004). Balancing marketing education and information technology: Matching needs or needing a better match? *Journal of Marketing Education, 26*, 75–88. http://dx.doi.org/10.1177/0273475303262350

Isaksen, G., & Ramberg, P. A. (2005, November). *Motivation and online learning*. Paper presented at the Interservice/Industry Training, Simulation, and Education Conference (I/ITSEC) 2005, Orlando, FL. Retrieved from http://brage.bibsys.no/xmlui/

Johnson, L., Adams, S., & Cummins, M. (2012). *NMC horizon report > 2012 higher education edition*. Retrieved from http://www.nmc.org/

Johnson, L., Adams Becker, S., Cummins, M., Estrada, V., Freeman, A., & Ludgate, H. (2013). *NMC horizon report > 2013 higher education edition*. Retrieved from http://www.nmc.org/

Johnson, S. D., & Aragon, S. R. (2003). An instructional strategy framework for online learning environments. *New Directions for Adult & Continuing Education, 2003*(100), 31–44. http://dx.doi.org/10.1002/ace.117

Jopling, M. (2009). *Online tuition: A literature review*. Retrieved from https://wlv.ac.uk/PDF/sed-res-becta-onlinetuition.pdf

Jopling, M. (2012). 1:1 online tuition: A review of the literature from a pedagogical perspective. *Journal of Computer Assisted Learning, 28*, 310–321. http://dx.doi.org/10.1111/j.1365-2729.2011.00441.x

Kersaint, G., Dogbey, J., Barber, J., & Kephart, D. (2011). The effect of access to an online tutorial service on college algebra student outcomes. *Mentoring & Tutoring, 19*, 25–44. http://dx.doi.org/10.1080/13611267.2011.543568

Kimberlin, C. L., & Winterstein, A. G. (2008). Validity and reliability of measurement instruments used in research. *American Journal of Health-System Pharmacy, 65*, 2276–2284. http://dx.doi.org/10.2146/ajhp070364

Little, B. B., Passmore, D., & Schullo, S. (2006). Using synchronous software in web-based nursing courses. *CIN: Computers, Informatics, Nursing, 24*, 317–325. http://dx.doi.org/10.1097/00024665-200611000-00005

Liu, S., Gomez, J., Khan, B., & Yen, C.-J. (2007). Toward a learner-oriented community college online course dropout framework. *International Journal on E-Learning, 6*, 519–542. Retrieved from http://www.editlib.org/j/IJEL/

Macintyre, R., & Macdonald, J. R. (2011). Remote from what? Perspectives of distance learning students in remote rural areas of Scotland. *International Review of Research in Open and Distance Learning, 12*(4), 1–16. Retrieved from http://www.irrodl.org/index.php/irrodl

Martinovic, D. (2009, May). Being an expert mathematics online tutor: What does expertise entail? *Mentoring & Tutoring: Partnership in Learning, 17*, 165–185. http://dx.doi.org/10.1080/13611260902860125

McBrien, J. L., Cheng, R., & Jones, P. (2009). Virtual spaces: Employing a synchronous online classroom to facilitate student engagement in online learning. *International Review of Research in Open and Distance Learning, 10*(3), Art. 6. Retrieved from http://www.irrodl.org/index.php/irrodl

McKechnie, L. (2008). Unstructured observation. In L. M. Given (Ed.), *The SAGE encyclopedia of qualitative research methods* (pp. 908–909). http://dx.doi.org/10.4135/9781412963909.n476

Means, B., Toyama, Y., Murphy, R., Bakia, M., & Jones, K. (2010). Evidence-based practices in online learning: A meta-analysis and review of online learning studies. Retrieved from http://www.ed.gov

Middle States Commission on Higher Education. (2011). *Distance education programs: Interregional guidelines for the evaluation of distance education (online learning)*. Retrieved from http://www.msche.org/publications/Guidelines-for-the-Evaluation-of-Distance-Education-Programs.pdf

Moore, M. G. (2007). The theory of transactional distance. In M. G. Moore (Ed.), *Handbook of distance education* (2nd ed., pp. 89–105). Mahwah, NJ: Erlbaum.

Moore, M. G. (Ed.). (2013). The theory of transactional distance. In *Handbook of distance education* (3rd ed., pp. 66–85). New York, NY: Routledge.

Moreno, R., & Mayer, R. (2007). Interactive multimodal learning environments. *Educational Psychology Review, 19*, 309–326. http://dx.doi.org/10.1007/s10648-007-9047-2

National Science Board. (2012). *Science and engineering indicators 2012* (NSB 12-01). Retrieved from http://www.nsf.gov

Ng, K. C. (2007). Replacing face-to-face tutorials by synchronous online technologies: Challenges and pedagogical implications. *International Reviews of Research in Open and Distance Learning, 8*(1), Art. 6. Retrieved from http://www.irrodl.org/index.php/irrodl

Ozkan, H. H. (2010). Cooperative learning technique through Internet based education: A model proposal. *Education, 130*, 499–508. Retrieved from http://www.projectinnovation.biz/education.html

Packham, G., Jones, P., Thomas, B., & Miller, C. (2006). Student and tutor perspectives of on-line moderation. *Education & Training, 48*, 241–251. http://dx.doi.org/10.1108/00400910610671915

Potacco, D. R. (2015). *A mixed method study of the adoption of online academic support by STEM students in higher education* (Doctoral dissertation). Retrieved from MARPs, Practicums and Applied Dissertations database. (11294)

Potacco, D. R., Chen, P., Desroches, D., Chisholm, D. R., & De Young, S. (2013). Coupons for student success: A marketing incentive in academic support. *The Learning Assistance Review, 18*(1),

28–45. Retrieved from http://www.nclca.org/tlar.html

Potacco, D. R., & De Young, S. (2007). The business of academic support. *The Learning Assistance Review, 12*(2), 19–31. Retrieved from http://www.nclca.org/tlar.html

Potacco, D. R., Orellana, A., Chen, P., & Salazar, A. (2016). Rethinking academic support: Improving the outcomes of students in high-risk STEM courses with synchronous videoconferencing. *Journal of College Student Retention: Research, Theory & Practice*, 1–20. http://dx.doi.org/10.1177/1521025116678854

Radford, A. W. (2011). *Learning at a distance: Undergraduate enrollment in distance education courses and degree programs* (NCES 2012154). Retrieved from http://nces.ed.gov

Rice, K. L. (2006). A comprehensive look at distance education in the K–12 context. *Journal of Research on Technology in Education, 38*, 425–448. http://dx.doi.org/10.1080/15391523.2006.10782468

Richardson, J. T. E. (2009). Face-to-face versus online tutoring support in humanities courses in distance education. *Arts and Humanities in Higher Education, 8*, 69–85. http://dx.doi.org/10.1177/1474022208098303

Rogers, E. M. (2003). *Diffusion of innovations* (5th ed.). New York, NY: Free Press.

Selvi, K. (2010). Motivating factors in online courses. *Procedia-Social and Behavioral Sciences, 2*, 819–824. http://dx.doi.org/10.1016/j.sbspro.2010.03.110

Shea, P., Pickett, A., & Li, C. S. (2005). Increasing access to higher education: A study of the diffusion of online teaching among 913 college faculty. *International Review of Research in Open and Distance Learning, 6*(2), Art. No. 3. Retrieved from http://www.irrodl.org/index.php/irrodl

Shelley, M., White, C., Baumann, U., & Murphy, L. (2006). "It's a unique role!" Perspectives on tutor attributes and expertise in distance language teaching. *International Review of Research in Open and Distance Learning, 7*(2), 1–15. Retrieved from http://www.irrodl.org/index.php/irrodl

Simonson, M. R. (2012). *An applied research agenda for instructional technology and distance education*. Retrieved from http://itde.nova.edu/Resources/uploads/app/43/files/itde/research-agenda-simonson.pdf

Simonson, M. R., Schlosser, C., & Orellana, A. (2011). Distance education research: A review of the literature. *Journal of Computing in Higher Education, 23,* 124–142. http://dx.doi.org/10.1007/s12528-011-9045-8

Smith, S. D., Salaway, G., & Caruso, J. B. (2009). *The ECAR study of undergraduate students and information technology, 2009.* Retrieved from https://net.educause.edu/research-and-publications

Sorensen, C. K., & Baylen, D. M. (2009). Learning online: Adapting the seven principles of good practice to a web-based instructional environment. In A. Orellana, T. K, Hudgins, & M. R. Simonson (Eds.), *The perfect online course: Best practices for designing and teaching* (pp. 69–86). Charlotte, NC: Information Age.

Stanford-Bowers, D. E. (2008). Persistence in online classes: A study of perceptions among community college stakeholders. *Journal of Online Learning and Teaching, 4,* 37–50. Retrieved from http://jolt.merlot.org/

Stickler, U., & Hampel, R. (2007). Designing online tutor training for language courses: A case study. *Open Learning, 22,* 75–85. http://dx.doi.org/10.1080/02680510601100176

Tallent-Runnels, M. K., Cooper, S., Lan, W. Y., Thomas, J. A., & Busby, C. (2005). How to teach online: What the research says. *Distance Learning, 2*(1), 21–27. Retrieved from http://www.infoagepub.com/distance-learning

Tallent-Runnels, M. K., Thomas, J. A., Lan, W. Y., Cooper, S., Ahern, T. C., Shaw, S. M., & Liu, X. (2006). Teaching courses online: A review of the research. *Review of Educational Research, 76,* 93–135. http://dx.doi.org/10.3102/00346543076001093

Tinto, V. (2006). Research and practice of student retention: What next? *Journal of College Student Retention: Research, Theory and Practice, 8,* 1–19. http://dx.doi.org/10.2190/4YNU-4TMB-22DJ-AN4W

Tossi, M. (2012, January 1). Labor force projections to 2020: A more slowly growing workforce. *Monthly Labor Review,* 43–64. Retrieved from http://www.bls.gov/opub/mlr

U.S. Department of Education, Office of Postsecondary Education. (2008). *Evidence of quality in distance education programs drawn from interviews with the accreditation community.* Retrieved from http://www.ysu.edu

U.S. Department of Education, National Center for Educational Statistics. (2011). *Web tables: Postsecondary awards in science, technology, engineering, and mathematics by state: 2001 and 2009* (NCES 2011-226). Retrieved from http://nces.ed.gov

U.S. Senate Committee on Health, Education, Labor & Pensions. (2012, July 30). *For profit higher education: The failure to safeguard the federal investment and ensure student success.* Retrieved from http://www.help.senate.gov

Wang, T. (2005). Tensions in learner support and tutor support in tertiary web-based English language education in China. *International Review of Research in Open and Distance Learning, 6*(3), Art. 9. Retrieved from http://www.irrodl.org/index.php/irrodl/index

Wejnert, B. (2002). Integrating models of diffusion of innovations: A conceptual framework. *Annual Review Sociology, 28,* 297–326. http://dx.doi.org/10.1146/annurev.soc.28.110601.141051

Wenger, E., White, N., Smith, J. D., & Rowe, K. (2005). *Technology for communities.* Retrieved from http://technologyforcommunities.com/CEFRIO_Book_Chapter_v_5.2.pdf

William Paterson University. (2015). *Fact book 2014–2015.* Retrieved from http://www.wpunj.edu/ira/FACTBOOKS/factbooks.dot

Wilson, B. G. (2012). Trends and issues facing distance education: A nowcasting exercise. In L. Visser, R. J. Amirault, & Y. L. Visser (Eds.), *Trends and issues in distance education: International perspectives* (2nd ed., pp. 39–54). Charlotte, NC: Information Age.

Zacharias, N. T. (2012). *Qualitative research methods for second language education: A coursebook.* Newcastle Upon Tyne, England: Cambridge Scholars.

AFFINITY SPACES IN HIGHER EDUCATION

Kelly McKenna
Colorado State University

The purpose of this mixed methods study was to determine what characteristics of affinity spaces are found in distance higher education. Affinity spaces have been established as successful learning environments, but as of yet, have not been established in distance higher education. Faculty and students from 3 cohorts of a distance educational studies doctoral program at a teaching-intensive university were surveyed. Data found that 83% of affinity space characteristics were encompassed in the learning space. Exploration of the space specific to contributions, diversity, and engagement are presented and discussed. Finally, the participants in the space are presented as a significant component in distance higher education affinity spaces.

INTRODUCTION

With 5.5 million students enrolled in distance education courses (U.S. Department of Education, 2014), there comes a responsibility by educators and educational institutions to deliver a quality experience for participants (Somenarain, Akkaraju, & Gharbaran, 2010). Creating an effective educational environment conducive to online student learning is imperative; however, research focused on creating an effective distance environment has been lacking in higher education. Available research highlights that affinity spaces can lead to a successful learning environment and experience (Beemt, Akkerman, & Simons, 2011; Brass, & Mecoli, 2011; Curwood, 2013; Fields, 2009; Gee, 2013).

James Paul Gee is known for establishing *affinity spaces* in literacy, gaming, and education literature (Gee, 2005, 2007, 2013). Affinity spaces are physical or virtual places where individuals with a shared interest gather to facilitate learning, gain collective intelligence, and produce artifacts related to a joint enterprise (Gee, 2005). Although Gee's (2005) research of affinity spaces stems from gaming, he stated that these social configurations have considerable implications for the future of schools and schooling. Gee (2013) acknowledged that "schools and colleges could have been and should be in the future a network of well-designed interacting affinity spaces devoted to synchronized intelligence" (p. 177). The notion that affinity spaces have implications in education is shared by experts in the

• **Kelly McKenna**, Colorado State University, 1588 Campus Delivery, Fort Collins, CO 80523. Telephone: (970) 491-5160. E-mail: Kelly.McKenna@colostate.edu

The Quarterly Review of Distance Education, Volume 18(3), 2017, pp. 19–32   ISSN 1528-3518

field (Beemt et al., 2011; Gee, 2005). Beemt et al. (2011) argued that:

> Social and cultural spaces are increasingly defined around affinities ... affinity spaces should not be set aside as something students deal with outside school hours. Instead ... an exploration of how education can connect to the affinity spaces that students engage in is necessary. (p. 63)

By connecting affinity spaces to education, students' academic careers are more aligned with their lives outside of academia, rather than expectations in these two areas being completely isolated (Gee, 2007).

In spite of the acknowledged connections between education and affinity spaces (Beemt et al., 2011; Gee, 2005, 2007) and the plethora of literature on affinity spaces in relation to gaming and digital literacy, research pertaining to the association of affinity spaces and education is lacking; research relating affinity spaces with the distance higher education setting is not specifically identified. With a focus on the learning space, affinity spaces align with distance education and its emphasis on the virtual learning space that is available anytime, anywhere. If a space incorporates numerous, but not all, of the features of an affinity space, it is essentially an affinity space (Gee, 2005). This research aimed to bridge the gap in literature connecting affinity spaces as successful learning environments to distance higher education as well as generating new knowledge regarding creating effective online learning environments and strove to reveal further necessary research arenas.

This article describes part of a larger mixed methods study focused on examining distance higher education learning spaces through the lens of affinity spaces. The scope of research presented here explored if distance higher education learning spaces are affinity spaces and if affinity spaces do, in fact, have implications in distance higher education. Online learning spaces were examined to establish if affinity spaces could be applied in distance higher education. The researcher agrees with Gee and others' declarations prioritizing the interactions of individuals in a learning space and the formation of affinity spaces in education (Beemt et al., 2011; Gee, 2007); however, prior to commencing the study, the researcher questioned whether a greater emphasis needed to be placed on the participants in the space when equating affinity spaces with distance higher education learning spaces.

RESEARCH QUESTIONS

The study sought to answer three research questions:

1. What characteristics of affinity spaces, as defined by Gee, are exhibited in distance higher education learning spaces?
2. Who contributes to the learning space in a distance higher education program?
3. How do graduate higher education learners utilize virtual spaces in distance education?

THEORETICAL FRAMEWORK

Affinity spaces guide the research and are understood to be places for learning where individuals gather "to share resources and values and flexibly form and re-form in different groups" (Gee, 2013, p. 174). Affinity spaces place an emphasis on the space where participants interact around a common enterprise (Gee, 2005). Participants may be diverse, but have a mutual interest in common and can engage in the space as deeply as wanted to gain as much expertise on the subject as they desire. Despite the presence of social interactions in the affinity space, Gee's (2005, 2013) research does not place an emphasis on participants of the space. Yet, the social phenomenon of learning is imperative to education (Rovai, Ponton, & Baker, 2008) and a focus of this study. Wenger's (1998) communities of practice place an emphasis on the members within the learning community and, thus, was used as a lens through which to view the participants in the affinity space, a necessity when exploring the distance higher education learning space.

Adult learners are a unique student population. The Flannery and Apps (1987) study of adult learners indicated that these students are balancing a variety of roles: student, family member, and employee, to name a few. They are required to balance a number of differing responsibilities, making *student* not their primary appointment (Flannery & Apps, 1987). Yet, participation by adults in formal higher education continues to escalate due to the potential for career advancement (Ginsberg & Wlodkowski, 2010). This division of responsibility leads adults to distance education. Adults are the most prevalent population in online learning (Ginsberg & Wlodkowski, 2010). The social learning theories of affinity space and communities of practice in combination with adult learning theory provided a complete framework for the study of learning spaces within a distance higher education program.

LITERATURE REVIEW

Both communities of practice and affinity spaces are created around a common enterprise. Participants may be diverse, but have some mutual interest in common. Also, both Wenger's (1998) communities of practice and Gee's (2005) affinity spaces can be real, virtual, or a hybrid. However, the fundamental components of the two vary slightly and the emphases of the two are distinctively unique.

Affinity Spaces

Gee (2005) addressed affinity spaces and communities of practice and presented affinity spaces as an alternative to communities of practice. Affinity spaces "focus on the idea of a *space* in which people interact, rather than on *membership* in a community" (Gee, 2013, p. 214). With membership, learning communities are more focused on the individuals that make up the community, rather than on the space or

place being "occupied." In affinity spaces, the emphasis is on the space (physical, virtual, or geographical) where individuals relate (Gee, 2013). This space is comprised of portals (access to the space) and generators (content). The focus should, therefore, be on the space and how it is utilized by different individuals (Henderson & Hirst, 2007). "These physical, virtual or blended spaces are often spread across many sites, such as face-to-face meetings, message boards, blogs and web pages" (Lammers, Curwood, & Magnifico, 2012).

Affinity spaces are "places where people can go to share resources and values and flexibly form and re-form in different groups" (Gee, 2013, p. 174). These spaces can be face-to-face, online, at a distance, or any combination of these. In affinity spaces, individuals gather around a shared passion (Gee, 2013). Participants in the space have the opportunity to become as involved as they want and to become an expert to the degree they desire. Affinity spaces provide a place where individuals congregate to be creative and generate a collective intelligence, created through contributions by all individuals, that is greater than the sum of its parts (Gee, 2013).

A review of affinity spaces established 18 characteristics (Gee, 2013). The presence of a majority of these characteristics indicates a learning space is essentially an affinity space.

Learning Spaces Human Element

Communities of practice focus on the social aspect of learning. Wenger (1998) acknowledged that these "communities" have been around for centuries and that he is simply implementing an innovative approach to theories of learning. He dictated that learning is in fact a social phenomenon, a "process of being active participants in the *practices* of social communities and constructing *identities* in relation to these communities" (Wenger, 1998, p. 4). The individuals that make up a community of practice are at the core of this learning theory. Communities of practice are "groups of people informally bound together by shared expertise and passion" (Wenger & Snyder, 2000, p. 139). The "space" is not an imperative element in communities of practice, rather who makes up the population is significant. The individuals in the community energize the community and "organize themselves ... and establish their own leadership" (Wenger & Snyder, 2000, p. 142).

MIXED METHOD STUDY

With an interest in fully exploring the distance education learning space, it was evident that a mixed method approach combining both quantitative and qualitative approaches most accurately supported the inquiry. For this research, the term mixed methods indicates Smith's (2009) definition, referring to "studies or projects that employ at least one quantitative and one qualitative method to produce knowledge claims" (p. 458). The purpose of the mixed method design used for this research was complementary. Employing both types of data seeks "elaboration, enhancement, illustration, [and] clarification of the results from one method with the results from the other method" (Greene, Caracelli, & Graham, 1989).

Both quantitative and qualitative data collected explored the distance higher education classroom. The quantitative data solely focused on the elements attributed to affinity spaces. The qualitative data consisted of open-ended questions relating to the learning space in distance higher education.

Participants and Setting

Participants were recruited from a single program at a university in the Rocky Mountain Region. The sample was a convenience sample of 45, comprised of 6 faculty and 39 doctoral students and had a response rate of 56% (3 faculty and 22 students). The program was a distance educational studies doctoral program that has initiated three cohorts since its inception. The 39 students who were contacted were students from all three cohorts, in varying

phases of the program (first year in the program, middle of the program, and completed the program). Participants in the study were located throughout the United States and internationally and ranged in age from 27–60.

The university was a midsize teaching intensive university in the Rocky Mountain Region with a graduate enrollment of 2,542 (University of Northern Colorado, 2015). According to the fall 2015 census, 40% of these students were enrolled in at least one online course; 57.8% of the graduate students were in The College of Education and Behavioral Sciences, which houses the Educational Studies EdD Program (University of Northern Colorado, 2015).

Data Collection

Participants in the study were sent online surveys through their university e-mail. Surveys contained 4-point Likert scale questions and open-ended questions requesting brief explanations. The Likert scale questions corresponded to the characteristics identified by Gee (2013) as necessary elements in an affinity space. This approach was utilized to provide a more comprehensive understanding (Creswell, 2014).

Data Analysis

A reflective journal was utilized for rudimentary analysis, a technique "to keep track of your thoughts, musings, speculations, and hunches as you engage in analysis. This kind of information might be interwoven with your raw data, or it may be separate files or memos" (Merriam, 1998, p. 165). The questionnaire was analyzed with both quantitative and qualitative approaches. SPSS was used for statistical analysis of the data collected from the Likert scale questions. A principal components analysis was completed on the 27 Likert scale questions linked to Gee's (2013) 18 characteristics of affinity spaces.

Responses to the open-ended questions in the questionnaire were coded for a systematic interpretation of the data (Remler & Van Ryzin, 2011). The primary intention of coding the data was for qualitative analysis. Coding is an iterative process through which themes in the data emerge (Creswell, 2014). Following coding of the responses and emergence of themes, the larger meaning, or interpretation, of the qualitative data is conceptualized (Creswell, 2013).

Validity and Reliability

Although quantitative methods were utilized in some of the analysis of data, the research was exploratory. An emphasis was placed on meticulous documentation of the analysis process, including steps taken and the motivations and logic behind the process. The use of triangulation, in particular through multiple forms of data collection and analysis, improves both internal validity and reliability in the research (Merriam, 1998). Data were collected from multiple perspectives and in a variety of modes. Also, multiple questions measure the same elements to ensure consistency in the data collected throughout the survey (Creswell, 2014).

FINDINGS AND DISCUSSION

For the purposes of this study, a learning space was defined as places individuals with a shared affinity assemble, face to face, online, or at a distance to: share resources and values, generate collective intelligence, and create collaborative artifacts. Gee (2005) indicated that if a space includes many of the characteristics of affinity spaces, then it is essentially an affinity space.

Affinity Space Characteristics

Current and former students of an educational studies distance program were asked to what degree on a 4-point Likert scale they agreed on 27 questions. The scale included: *strongly agree* (1), *agree* (2), *disagree* (3), and

strongly disagree (4). The questions aligned with Gee's (2013) characteristics of affinity spaces. Table 1 depicts participants' responses on how affinity space characteristics aligned with their learning space.

It should be noted that, when the mean scores were combined to equate with their corresponding affinity space characteristics, there were only three characteristics of affinity spaces that student participants did not feel were evidenced in their learning space: participants' tenure in the space varied; because affinity spaces are created around an interest, there is no delineation between work and play within the space; and affinity spaces are based on empirical evidence, not assertions or philosophies. The remaining 15 characteristics of affinity spaces all received mean scores in the *agree* to *strongly agree* range (1–2).

Distance Higher Education Affinity Spaces

Gee (2005) stated that although there is potential for transforming education to more closely parallel affinity spaces, current students, teachers, and classrooms rarely align with many of the features he presented. However, the elements specific to online and higher education students can be effectively associated with an affinity space. The typical class segregates students by age (Gee, 2005), but in the educational studies distance higher education program, students ages varied from 27–60, and they were geographically dispersed. Unlike in a K–12 classroom, higher education learners vary greatly. Participants in the space either agreed or strongly agreed with a mean score of 1.37 that the cohort was comprised of individuals with diverse backgrounds. Adults come to education environments with diverse and disproportionate prior experience (Long, 2004). Agreement with this was reflected in the data from participants in this study who agreed that individuals in the cohort range from amateurs to experts in educational studies. This diversity in age, background, and level of expertise was consistent with partici-

TABLE 1
Descriptive Statistics

Statement	Mean	SD	Analysis N
You are in the educational studies learning space by choice.	1.11	.315	19
You have a shared interest with the other students in your educational studies cohort.	1.11	.315	19
The educational studies cohort is comprised of individuals with diverse backgrounds.	1.37	.496	19
The educational studies cohort is comprised of individuals of varying ages.	1.32	.582	19
Individuals in the cohort range from amateurs to experts in educational studies.	1.89	.658	19
The individuals in the cohort have a variety of interests surrounding education.	1.32	.478	19
High standards for excellence within the learning space are set by individuals with mastery of the content.	1.58	.607	19
The learning space is dedicated to production not just the gathering of knowledge.	1.63	.597	19
All members of the learning space have the opportunity to contribute to the degree they are interested.	1.63	.496	19
All contributions to the learning space have potential for significance.	1.58	.507	19
All contributions to the learning space are welcome.	1.58	.692	19
Diversity within the learning space is valued.	1.58	.607	19
Status within the learning space is amenable and fluid.	1.63	.496	19
Leadership within the learning space is amenable and fluid.	1.79	.631	19
Status in the cohort is based on an individual's engagement and accomplishments within the learning space, not what has been attained outside of the space.	2.00	.745	19
Resources within the learning space are plentiful. (e.g. peers, experts, outside materials, content links....)	1.89	.937	19
Resources within the learning space are fluid and amendable by the participants rather than static resources.	1.79	.631	19
Participants in learning space may have a specific focus, but must also collaborate with others.	1.53	.513	19
The learning space has established a unique culture.	1.26	.452	19
The learning space is open to new ideas and recognizes outside knowledge to ensure growth and diversity.	1.37	.496	19
All individuals in the learning space are expected to facilitate learning for themselves and other participants.	1.63	.684	19
Participants' motivations in the learning space vary.	1.58	.607	19
Participants' tenure in the learning space varies.	2.11	.737	19
Because participants in the cohort have a shared interest there is no delineation between mandatory participation and intrinsic enrichment within the learning space.	2.37	.761	19
Socialization within the learning space is secondary only to the objective of the learning space.	2.21	.855	19
Socialization within the learning space is achieved through a variety of mediums.	1.79	.631	19
The learning space is based on tangible production not assertions or philosophies.	2.05	.705	19

pant characteristics in Gee's (2013) affinity spaces. All participants, with the exception of one, agreed that diversity within the learning space is valued. Students in the online higher education course strongly agreed that they were brought together over a common interest, but their reasons for returning to school often varied greatly. Entry in an affinity space is for different reasons; it is simply the common endeavor that brings the individuals together (Gee, 2013). Of student participants, 95% agreed or strongly agreed that their motivations in the space varied greatly, and a mean score of 1.31 indicated that they had a variety of interest surrounding education.

In traditional teacher-centered learning, the teacher is entirely in control, dictating what students will learn, how the students will learn, and if the students have learned (Weimer, 2013). This control and delineation between students and teachers is contradictory to affinity spaces.

> In an affinity space, leadership and status are flexible. People sometimes lead and mentor; sometimes they follow and are mentored. There are no fixed bosses and teachers, though people acknowledge different paths to mastery and know where people are on them. (Gee, 2013, p. 176)

However, in adult education, the professor is encouraged to be a facilitator (Merriam, Caffarella, & Baumgartner, 2007). The idea of facilitating learning more closely aligns with Gee's (2005) affinity spaces. In this study, 89% of the students in the educational studies program either strongly agreed or agreed that all individuals in the learning space were expected to facilitate learning for themselves and others. An educator of adults has "many roles within the teaching and learning interaction including role model, mentor, counselor, content resource person, learning guide, instructional developer, and institutional representative" (Galbraith, 2004, p. 5). This relationship is more give and take and, therefore, more representative of an affinity space. In formal online adult education, the students are

often encouraged to "take charge" and assist in the instruction. Ninety-five percent of responses in this study indicated that status in the learning space is amenable and fluid, and 85% believed that leadership is also amenable and fluid. Learning in distance education is no longer a passive activity. A mean score of 1.58 was received, indicating that all contributions to the learning space are welcome and have potential for significance.

The distance classroom setting focuses on the education space, similar to affinity spaces that are often positioned in multiple locations (Lammers et al., 2012). Online classrooms are often launched on a learning management system containing discussion boards, chat rooms, group hangouts, and assignment and content resources. The survey statement that resources within the learning space are plentiful garnered a mean score of 1.89, indicating the participants agreed. Ninety percent of responses specified that the resources within the learning space are fluid and amendable by the participants, rather than static resources. Additional portals (Gee, 2005) are often created for collaboration between participants. Of participants in the educational studies learning space, 95% agreed or strongly agreed that they were required to collaborate with others. Learners often connect on social media, Google documents, wikis, and so forth, a list that continues to grow as technology advances. Similar to education classroom spaces that expand to external resources, affinity spaces link to other related spaces so that knowledge from the outside can transform the space (Gee, 2013). A mean score of 1.37 in this study indicated that the learning space was open to new ideas and recognized outside knowledge. Gee's (2013) focus on space creates the potential for a formal learning space to be considered an affinity space (Bommarito, 2014).

Variable Reduction

The variable reduction technique known as principal components analysis was used to analyze questions on the survey related to the

18 characteristics of affinity spaces. Due to the smaller size of this study and the number of questions analyzed, this technique was more advantageous than other variable reduction techniques (Dunteman, 1989; Field, 2005). Although due to the limited participant sample, all outcomes were supported by qualitative data. In addition, this procedure was utilized because it was believed that the variables in the characteristics were highly correlated. By completing a principal components analysis, these highly correlated variables can be reduced down to a small set of uncorrelated principal components by measuring the underlying constructs within the questions (Dunteman, 1989). A principal components analysis was run in SPSS to discover these underlying similarities in the 27 Likert scale questions that were included in the survey. These 27 questions related to the 18 items identified by Gee (2013) as characteristics of an affinity space. When the analysis was originally run, eight principal components were extracted from the data and accounted for 85.10% of the variance. The first principal component accounted for 33.46% of the variance within the variables. This original analysis of the data can be found in Table 2.

The output from SPSS was examined to determine what strategies would be most useful to further study the data. Dunteman (1989) acknowledged that there are several methods for determining how many components to retain, and these include the use of a scree plot and accounting for a desired percent of variance. This study was exploratory in nature, so a variety of variations to the analysis were attempted. Based on the scree plot, it was determined that it would be beneficial to extract four to five components as this was where the "elbow" of the plot was located (Field, 2005). The components settled within the steep portion of the line connecting components are preserved (Dunteman, 1989). The scree plot illustrated in Figure 1 represents this graphically.

Although the scree plot indicated that four to five principal components may be ideal, further investigation and analyses within SPSS ultimately led to the extraction of three principal components. Modifications including: the use of promax versus varimax, which indicates the items to extract if they were sufficiently similar, and the number of optimal components were all investigated. Table 3 displays the optimal principal component analysis with rotation method varimax with Kaiser normalization.

TABLE 2
Total Variance Explained

Component	Initial Eigenvalues			Extraction Sums of Squared Loadings		
	Total	% of Variance	Cumulative %	Total	% of Variance	Cumulative %
1	9.034	33.458	33.458	9.034	33.458	33.458
2	3.673	13.605	47.063	3.673	13.605	47.063
3	2.802	10.379	57.442	2.802	10.379	57.442
4	2.375	8.795	66.237	2.375	8.795	66.237
5	1.470	5.443	71.680	1.470	5.443	71.680
6	1.321	4.894	76.574	1.321	4.894	76.574
7	1.256	4.654	81.228	1.256	4.654	81.228
8	1.047	3.876	85.104	1.047	3.876	85.104
9	.829	3.071	88.175			

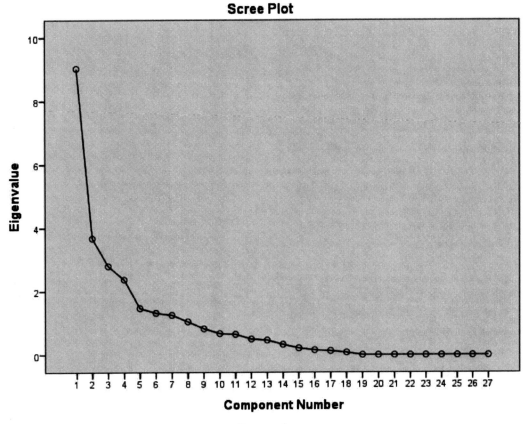

FIGURE 1
Scree Plot

Components

A thorough examination of the questions contained within each of the components was completed to determine the themes for each component. The three principal components include: (a) contributions to the space; (b) diversity within the space; and (c) engagement in the space. Table 4 was created to align affinity space characteristic, survey questions, and principal components. Column 1 lists each of the 18 characteristics Gee (2013) recognized as features of affinity spaces. Column 2 indicates which survey questions support each of Gee's characteristics. And finally, column 3 displays the component that each question was associated with based on the principal components analysis.

Diversity within the space was included in the discussion above concerning participants (instructors and students) in affinity spaces and the affinity space classroom. The components or themes of contributions to the space and engagement in the space were further explored through open-ended questions asked of both faculty and students. Both faculty and students of the learning space contributed to the space. This was achieved through the collaborative creation of the space and collective creation of the content within the space. One response indicated, "We all create the learning space. The instructor has a strong input in this design, but the students contribute and create the space through each course and provide a thread that weaves through all the courses through our shared work and group projects." The learning

TABLE 3
Rotated Component Matrix

Item	Component 1	2	3
All members of the learning space have the opportunity to contribute to the degree they are interested.	.887		
All contributions to the learning space have potential for significance.	.867		
Status within the learning space is amenable and fluid.	.858		
Leadership within the learning space is amenable and fluid.	.837		
High standards for excellence within the learning space are set by individuals with mastery of the content.	.761		
Diversity within the learning space is valued.	.753		
The learning space is open to new ideas and recognizes outside knowledge to ensure growth and diversity.	.752	.421	
All contributions to the learning space are welcome.	.752		
Status in the cohort is based on an individual's engagement and accomplishments within the learning space, not what has been attained outside of the space.	.687		
Individuals in the cohort range from amateurs to experts in educational studies.	.677		.344
The learning space is dedicated to production not just the gathering of knowledge.	.659		.302
Resources within the learning space are fluid and amendable by the participants rather than static resources.	.612	.554	
All individuals in the learning space are expected to facilitate learning for themselves and other participants.	.536	.400	−.309
The learning space has established a unique culture.	.481	.381	
Socialization within the learning space is secondary only to the objective of the learning space.		.761	
Because participants in the cohort have a shared interest there is no delineation between mandatory participation and intrinsic enrichment within the learning space.	−.324	.686	
The Educational Studies cohort is comprised of individuals with diverse backgrounds.		.648	
Resources within the learning space are plentiful (e.g., peers, experts, outside materials, content links).	.385	.647	−.327
Participants in learning space may have a specific focus, but must also collaborate with others.		.616	.388
The Educational Studies cohort is comprised of individuals of varying ages.		.578	
Participants' tenure in the learning space varies.	−.349	.492	
You have a shared interest with the other students in your Educational Studies cohort.		−.319	
Participants' motivations in the learning space vary.			.776
Socialization within the learning space is achieved through a variety of mediums.			.652
You are in the Educational Studies learning space by choice.		−.303	−.628
The learning space is based on tangible production not assertions or philosophies.	.574		.608
The individuals in the cohort have a variety of interests surrounding education.	.301		.496

TABLE 4
Affinity Space Component Alignment

Characteristic	Question	Components
1. People are in them by choice, based on a shared enterprise.	1. You are in the Educational Studies learning space by choice. 2. You have a shared interest with the other students in your Educational Studies cohort.	• Diversity • Engagement
2. Participants in the affinity space are of diverse ages and backgrounds.	3. The Educational Studies cohort is comprised of individuals with diverse backgrounds. 4. The Educational Studies cohort is comprised of individuals of varying ages.	• Diversity
3. Individuals range from amateurs to experts in the common endeavor of the space.	5. Individuals in the cohort range from amateurs to experts in educational studies.	• Contributions • Engagement
4. Interest in the subject matter of the affinity space can vary greatly.	6. The individuals in the cohort have a variety of interests surrounding education.	• Contributions • Engagement
5. High standards for excellence in the enterprise are set by individuals with mastery of the content.	7. High standards for excellence within the learning space are set by individuals with mastery of the content.	• Contributions
6. Affinity spaces are dedicated to producing and knowledge.	8. The learning space is dedicated to production not just the gathering of knowledge.	• Contributions • Engagement
7. All members have the opportunity to contribute to the degree they are interested and each contribution has potential for significance in the affinity space.	9. All members of the learning space have the opportunity to contribute to the degree they are interested. 10. All contributions to the learning space have potential for significance.	• Contributions
8. All contributions to the space are welcome and diversity is valued.	11. All contributions to the learning space are welcome. 12. Diversity within the learning space is valued.	• Contributions
9. Status within the affinity space and leadership are amenable and fluid.	13. Status within the learning space is amenable and fluid. 14. Leadership within the learning space is amenable and fluid.	• Contributions
10. Status is based on an individual's engagement and accomplishments within the space, not what has been attained outside of the space.	15. Status in the cohort is based on an individual's engagement and accomplishments within the learning space, not what has been attained outside of the learning space.	• Contributions
11. Resources within the space are plentiful and are amended by the participants in the affinity space.	16. Resources within the learning space are plentiful (e.g., peers, experts, outside materials, content links). 17. Resources within the learning space are fluid and amendable by the participants rather than static resources.	• Contributions • Diversity • Engagement
12. Participants in affinity spaces may have a specific focus, but must also collaborate with others in the space.	18. Participants in learning space may have a specific focus, but must also collaborate with others.	• Diversity • Engagement
13. Each affinity space has a marked culture, but acknowledges outside knowledge to ensure growth and diversity.	19. The learning space has established a unique culture. 20. The learning space is open to new ideas and recognizes outside knowledge to ensure growth and diversity.	• Contributions • Diversity

(Table continues on next page)

TABLE 4
(Continued)

Characteristic	Question	Components
14. All individuals in the affinity space are expected to facilitate learning for themselves and other participants.	21. All individuals in the learning space are expected to facilitate learning for themselves and other participants.	• Contributions • Diversity • Engagement
15. Participants' motivations and tenure in the space varies.	22. Participants motivations in the learning space vary. 23. Participants tenure in the learning space varies.	• Contributions • Diversity • Engagement
16. Because affinity spaces are created around an interest there is no delineation between work and play within the space.	24. Because participants in the cohort have a shared interest there is no delineation between mandatory participation and intrinsic enrichment within the learning space.	• Contributions • Diversity
17. Socialization is secondary only to the venture of the affinity space and is achieved through a variety of mediums.	25. Socialization within the learning space is secondary only to the objective of the learning space. 26. Socialization within the learning space is achieved through a variety of mediums.	• Diversity • Engagement
18. Affinity spaces are based on empirical evidence not assertions or philosophies.	27. The learning space is based on tangible production not assertions or philosophies.	• Contributions • Engagement

space is comprised of a multitude of portals. One faculty member described this as a web. Portals are how the space is accessed (Gee, 2005). In the case of the distance doctoral program, these portals included Blackboard, wikis, Facebook pages, Skype, and so forth. Contributions to the space in the form of content or generators (Gee, 2005) are, again, created by all involved in the space. As noted in the characteristics of affinity spaces, sometimes this is completed collectively, and sometimes these are individual contributions. It should also be noted that responses often indicated that some of the spaces within the Distance Educational Studies Affinity Space were accessible only to students, not faculty. In addition to contributing to the "physical" aspects of the space, participants also created the culture and environment of the space, explaining it was "social, supportive, welcoming, fun, safe, [and] collaborative."

One participant articulated a sentiment that was pervasive throughout the research regarding the learning space, saying they "are created to facilitate collaboration, socialization, and production of educational ideas and materi-

als." Or, "the learning space is characterized by motivated like-minded people seeking an advancement in their educational careers." These descriptions aligned with the characteristics and definition of affinity spaces as places where individuals with a shared interest gather to facilitate learning, gain collective intelligence, and produce artifacts related to a joint enterprise (Gee, 2005). Participants in this study noted several reasons they engaged in the space: social interactions/communications, collaboration, sharing resources, questions/clarification, academic and emotional support, and for assignments. With the exception of engaging in the space for assignments, the focus was on connections between the participants in the space. This was not surprising as research supports the notion that in online education, there is a greater need for interaction and communication in order for students to succeed (Rovai et al., 2008). When students were asked to what degree they agreed with the following statement, "Socialization within the space is secondary only to the objective of the learning space," the mean score of 2.21 disagreed with the statement. However, one student's comment perfectly articulated this characteristic, "learning is at the core of the learning space, but the ability to socialize and interact is a key contributor to the effectiveness of the learning space." Another participant described the learning space as "social, constant connections with peers."

Learning Space Participants

Throughout this research studying the learning space, participants' emphasis was on the other individuals in the space including their interactions, connections, collaborations, support etc. The space was used to "share and ask for educational resources, and vent frustrations as well as announce accomplishments [and] we push each others' thinking by reflecting on our homework assignment readings, our own personal experiences … prior knowledge." Kasl and Yorks (2016) discussed learning, stating that "by presenting ideas to others and encountering others' points of view, learners clarify, expand, and attune their thinking" (p. 4). One participant in the space even told the story of how they would often utilize Skype all day with another individual in the program, regardless of whether or not they were working together. It was left on even when they might temporarily leave or take a nap; the intent was simply for the connection with someone else from the learning space. Of the three cohorts to go through the program, one cohort graduated almost 2 years earlier and, yet, they still continued relationships and connections, collaborated, and maintained various portals in their affinity space. One student from this cohort described their learning space as "sustainable, even today we still have learning spaces in place long after we all have graduated." Without the participants and their engagement in the learning space, it would cease to exist.

IMPLICATIONS AND FUTURE RESEARCH

This study indicated that distance higher education learning spaces are, in fact, a series of interacting affinity spaces leading to effective education. However, this potential for optimal learning is only present when the space accentuates the participants. The participants in the space must contribute to the space and be actively engaged in the space, and there must be diversity within the space. Previous literature differentiated affinity spaces from communities of practice by focusing on the space, rather than the members in the space (Gee, 2005). But, in the educational studies distance higher education program, the participants in the space were an integral element of the affinity space. They were repeatedly described as the ultimate stakeholders within the space.

Due to the limited sample utilized in this study, future research on a variety of distance higher education programs could further investigate the participants in the space and their necessity in distance higher education affinity spaces. In addition, extended exploration of higher education learning spaces could ensure that the characteristics necessary for affinity spaces are present to ensure effective learning. In gaming, there may not be a need to emphasize the participants in an affinity space, but based on this research of distance higher education, one would be remiss to not accentuate the members in the space.

REFERENCES

Beemt, A. V. D., Akkerman, S., & Simons, R. J. (2011). Considering young people's motives for interactive media use. *Educational Research Review, 6,* 55–66.

Bommarito, D. (2014). Tending to change: Toward a situated model of affinity spaces. *E-Learning and Digital Media, 11*(4), 406–417.

Brass, J., & Mecoli, S. (2011). The (failed) case of the Winston Society wikispace: The challenges and opportunities of Web 2.0 and teacher education. *Contemporary Issues in Technology and Teacher Education, 11*(2), 149–166.

Creswell, J. W. (2013). *Qualitative inquiry and research design: Choosing among five approaches* (3rd ed.). Los Angeles, CA: SAGE.

Creswell, J. W. (2014). *Educational research: Planning, conducting, and evaluating quantita-*

tive and qualitative research (4th ed.). Upper Saddle River, NJ: Prentice Hall.

Curwood, J. S. (2013). The Hunger Games: Literature, literacy, and online affinity spaces. *Language Arts, 90*(6), 417–427.

Dunteman, G. H. (1989). *Principal components analysis*. Newbury Park, CA: SAGE.

Field, A. (2005). Principal component analysis. In A. Field (Ed.), *Discovering statistics using SPSS* (pp. 619–680). Thousand Oaks, CA: SAGE.

Fields, D. A. (2009, January). What do students gain from a week at science camp? Youth perceptions and the design of an immersive, research-oriented astronomy camp. *International Journal of Science Education, 31*(2), 151–171.

Flannery, D., & Apps, J. (1987). Characteristics and problems of older returning students. Retrieved from ERIC database. (ED296084)

Galbraith, M. W. (2004). The teacher of adults. In M. W. Galbraith (Ed.), *Adult learning methods: A guide for effective instruction* (3rd ed., pp. 3–21). Malabar, FL: Kreiger.

Gee, J. P. (2005). Semiotic social spaces and affinity spaces: From the age of mythology to today's schools. In D. Barton & K. Tusting (Eds.), *Beyond communities of practice: Language, power and social context* (pp. 214–232). New York, NY: Cambridge University Press.

Gee, J. P. (2007). *Good video games + good learning: Collected essays on video games, learning and literacy*. New York, NY: Peter Lang.

Gee, J. P. (2013). The anti-education era: Creating smarter students through digital learning. New York, NY: Palgrave Macmillan.

Ginsberg, M. B., & Wlodkowski, R. J. (2010). Access and participation. In C. E. Kasworm, A.D. Rose, & J. M. Ross-Gordon (Eds.), *Handbook of adult and continuing education* (pp. 25–34). Los Angeles, CA: SAGE.

Greene, J. C., Cracelli, V. J., & Graham, W. F. (1989). Toward a conceptual framework for mixed-method evaluation designs. *Education Evaluation and Policy Analysis, 11*(3), 255–274.

Henderson, R., & Hirst, E. (2007). Reframing academic literacy: Re-examining a short course for "disadvantaged" tertiary students. *English Teaching: Practice and Critique, 6*(2), 25–38.

Kasl, E., & Yorks, L. (2016). Do I really know you? Do you really know me? Empathy amid diversity in differing learning contexts. *Adult Education Quarterly, 66*(1), 3–20.

Lammers, J. C., Curwood, J. S., & Magnifico, A. M. (2012). Toward an affinity space methodology: Considerations for literacy research. *English Teaching: Practice and Critique, 11*(2), 44–58.

Long, H. B. (2004). Understanding adult learners. In M. W. Galbraith (Ed.), *Adult learning methods: A guide for effective instruction* (3rd ed.) (pp. 23–37). Malabar, FL: Kreiger.

Merriam, S. B. (1998). *Qualitative research and case study applications in education*. San Francisco, CA: Jossey-Bass.

Merriam, S. B., Cafferella, R. S., & Baumgartner, L. M. (2007). *Learning in adulthood* (3rd ed.). San Francisco, CA: Jossey-Bass.

Remler, D. K., & Van Ryzin, G. G. (2011). *Research methods in practice: Strategies for description and causation*. Los Angeles, CA: SAGE.

Rovai, A. P., Ponton, M. K., & Baker, J. D. (2008). *Distance learning in higher education: A programmatic approach to planning, instruction, evaluation, and accreditation*. New York, NY: Teachers College Press.

Smith, M. L. (2009). Multiple methodology in education research. In J. L. Green, G. Camilli, & P. B. Elmore (Eds.), *Handbook of complementary methods in education research* (pp. 457–475). New York, NY: Routledge.

Somenarain, L., Akkaraju, S., & Gharbaran R. (2010). Student perceptions and learning outcomes in asynchronous and synchronous online learning environments in a biology course. *Journal of Online Learning and Teaching, 6*(2), 353–356.

University of Northern Colorado. (2015). *2015 fall census* [PDF document]. Retrieved from http://www.unco.edu/iras/PDF's/Fall%202015%20Census%20-%209-17-15.pdf

U.S. Department of Education. (2014). *Enrollment in distance education courses, by state: Fall 2012* [PDF document]. Retrieved from http://nces.ed.gov/pubs2014/2014023.pdf

Weimer, M. (2013). *Learner-centered teaching: Five key changes to practice* (2nd ed.). San Francisco, CA: Jossey-Bass.

Wenger, E. (1998). *Communities of practice: Learning, meaning, and identity*. Cambridge, England: Cambridge University Press.

Wenger, E. C., & Snyder, W. M. (2000, January–February). Communities of practice: The organizational frontier. *Harvard Business Review*, 139–145.

CONCEPTUALIZING FORMAL AND INFORMAL LEARNING IN MOOCS AS ACTIVITY SYSTEMS

Kathlyn Bradshaw
Algonquin College

Gale Parchoma
University of Saskatchewan

Jennifer Lock
University of Calgary

This article considers formal and informal learning activities in massive open online courses (MOOCs). MOOCs are often broadly positioned as either cMOOCs (based on connectivistic pedagogies) or xMOOCs (based on cognitivistic/behavioristic pedagogies). In a recent *International Review of Research in Open and Distance* article, Anders (2015) proposed a tripartite scheme for placing MOOCs on a continuum from content-based (xMOOCs) to community/task-based (cMOOCs) to network-based hybrids. Anders' model is based on a meta-analysis of literature-based case studies of existing pedagogical approaches in MOOCs. In contrast, our in situ case study examined an emergent, hybrid MOOC design. The study shared in this article is focused on establishing the presence of both formal and informal learning activities in a network-based hybrid approach to MOOC design. The establishment of these two activity systems extended to include opportunities for boundary crossings between them. An outcome is a cultural-historical activity theory-informed model that extends commonly used and recognized MOOC typologies.

MOOCS

MOOCs can be defined as larger class sizes, available online to almost anyone, and involving learning objectives, assignments, and evaluation. Two primary approaches to MOOCs are cMOOCs (based on connectivistic pedagogies) and xMOOCs (based on cognitivistic/behavioristic pedagogies). xMOOCs can be seen as instances "where traditional institutions use online platforms to extend access to onsite learning activities, resources, and events, typically based upon the trans-mission of content and verification of reception model" (O'Toole, 2013, p. 2). O'Toole (2013) upholds xMOOCs and cMOOCs as not only distinct, but as "extremes" (p. 1). However, "basic pedagogical approaches are very similar": course materials are held in "a hub or central repository," learners participate "through online forums, study groups, and (in Coursera and Udacity) organized meetings," and automated software is often used to assess learner performances on quizzes or other assignments (Johnson et al., 2013, p. 12).

• **Kathlyn Bradshaw**, Professor, School of Business, Algonquin College, RM: 235s, 1385 Woodroffe Avenue B417. Ottawa, ON K2G 1V8. Telephone: (613) 727-4723 ext. 5891. E-mail: bradshk@algonquincollege.com

The Quarterly Review of Distance Education, Volume 18(3), 2017, pp. 33–50   ISSN 1528-3518

Learning Activity in MOOCs

Participants in either form of MOOC are identified as more self-directed (McAuley, Stewart, Siemans, & Cormier, 2010) than those involved in other types of online learning. Participants engage in "informal consumption, creation, communication and sharing of knowledge" (Selwyn & Simons, 2009, p. 2). MOOC participants are often portrayed as self-reflective, producing "self-generated thoughts, feelings and actions that are planned and cyclically adapted to the attainment of personal goals" (Littlejohn, 2013). They "self-organize their participation according to learning goals, prior knowledge and skills, and common interests" (McAuley et al., 2010 p. 4). Participants' learning experiences are claimed to be influenced by a MOOC design's tendency to "flatten hierarchy by allowing and forcing personal connection across the boundaries between teachers and learners in traditional academic and professional circles" (McCauley et al., 2010, p. 37). This latter phenomenon can arise most noticeably in that MOOCs often include a peer-evaluation system (O'Toole, 2013).

Haber (2014) typified xMOOCs as "the same lectures, reading and homework assignment, assessments, and discussions you would find in a traditional college class" (p. 47). xMOOCs tend towards formality "where learning is aligned to planned outcomes from an accredited curriculum and organized by a teacher who has a hierarchical relationship with students" (Wright, Short, & Parchoma, 2013, p. 54). Learning goals are typically defined by the teacher, and learning pathways are set within a bounded environment (Littlejohn, 2013). cMOOCs have been seen to follow "connectivist principles, where large numbers of participants self-assemble collections of knowledge, learning activities and curriculum from openly available sources across publically open platforms" (O'Toole, 2013).

PEDAGOGY, ANDROGOGY, AND HEUTAGOGY

Anders (2015) argued that distinctions among pedagogical, androgogical, and heutogogical assumptions about teaching and learning processes are salient to categorizing MOOCs. He defined pedagogical approaches as inherently evoking "instructor control" (p. 45), involving highly structured content and tasks that allow for few, if any, opportunities for individual learner autonomy or self-direction. In contrast, androgogical approaches allow groups of learners to negotiate pathways to achieving "skills and competencies" with their instructor. Heutogogical approaches promote "self-determined learning" in crowds or networks for the purposes of achieving "higher-order capabilities" and "critical thinking" (p. 45). While Anders' distinctions are valuable conceptual tools, his definition of pedagogy seems to be focused on behavioristic and cognitivistic pedagogical perspectives.

Behavioristic and Cognitivistic Perspectives on Pedagogy

A key tenet of behaviorism is "the principality of the individual (and her/his physical presence—i.e., brain-based) in learning" (Kowch, 2004, p. 87). Behavioralist explanations of the individual mind asks us to perceive cause-effect chains of environmental stimuli and embodied responses (Skinner, 1938). Learning then becomes a "direct reaction to the task set before a learner" (Vygotsky, 1978, p. 39). Behavioristic pedagogies focus on the efficient design of learning tasks and measurements of learning outcomes. Comparatively, cognitivistic pedagogies focus on logical ordering of content to be learned, tasks to be undertaken, and measures of outcomes. From a cognitivist perspective, the human mind is conceptualized as a system (Markauskaite & Goodyear, 2017) rather than an unseen intermediary between a stimulus and a response. From a cognitivist perspective, an individual's mind operates "as central control mechanism capable of abstraction, goal-setting, and imagination" where cognitions are "system-bound functions and processes that enable thoughts, decision-making, and action" (Parchoma, in press). Both behavioristic and cognitivistic accounts of human learning focus on accurate replication of received knowledge within the confines of an isolated mind. Neither account provides a comprehensive picture of learning processes.

> As Barsalou, Breazeal, and Smith (2007) have argued, cognition cannot be fully understood as limited to a collection of processes operating within a closed system because cognitive processes must coordinate with other internal (embodied) and external (socio-cultural and environmental) systems. (Parchoma, in press)

Pedagogical approaches that focus on either behavioristic or cognitivistic perspectives of learning lack considerations for sociocultural and environmental influences on learning processes. They fail to address possibilities for emergent knowledge.

Connectivistic Perspectives on Pedagogy

Connectivism involves "a more individualized or personalized perspective on learning" (Ryberg, Buus, & Georgeson, 2012, p. 51). Connectivism is "a pedagogy in which knowledge is not a destination but an ongoing activity, fueled by the relationships people build and the deep discussions catalyzed within" (Johnson et al., 2013, p. 11). Where behaviorism focuses primarily on what is internal to a learner, connectivism addresses "learning that occurs outside of people" (Siemens, 2005, para. 12). Downes (2017) argued that, "knowledge is itself a set of connections in network, a pattern of connectivity.... Learning therefore needs to be active, it needs to be networked-based, and it needs to be constituted essentially of interactions between networks of users" (p. 12).

Instructional designers following connectivism are more likely to design tasks focused on "connecting specialized information sets" (Siemens, 2005, para. 16), within "a more individualized or personalised perspective on learning" (Ryberg, Buus, & Georgsen, 2011, p. 51). cMOOCs may involve "software tools for discovery, connection, and cocreation" (Milligan, Littlejohn, & Margaryan, 2013, p. 150). Within connectivism, goals for learning "tend to be defined by the learner … learning pathways are open and ill defined … and interaction with others is expected but has to be initiated by the learner" (Littlejohn, 2013). Learning in cMOOCs can thus be identified as having "informal, incidental, learner-initiated activities" (Wright et al., 2013, p. 54).

Constructivist Perspectives on Pedagogy

Constructivist theory, most closely aligned with our work, draws on personal experience and contextualizes it: "the individual human subject engaging with objects in the world and making sense of them" (Crotty, 2010, p. 79). From a constructivist perspective, learning can be seen as "a negotiation between individual and social knowledge, whose contributions have a dialectical relationship and cannot be meaningfully separated" (Karagiorgi & Symeou, 2005, p. 18). Karagiorgi and Symeou (2005) argued that student-centered instructional environments would include authentic tasks and are supported through teacher scaffolding. In a constructivist learning environment, approaches such as the following are used: "situated cognition, cognitive apprenticeship, anchored instruction and cooperative learning" (p. 18). Learning emerges from the interaction between learners and the world around them.

CULTURAL-HISTORICAL ACTIVITY THEORY

Cultural-historical activity theory (CHAT) gives weight to cultural, historical, as well as technological human activity. Activity theory "provides an effective lens for analyzing tasks and settings" (Jonassen & Rohrer-Murphy, 1999, p. 222). It provides a system to support the conceptualization of formal and informal learning as activity systems. The assumptions of CHAT "are consonant with those of constructivism" (Jonassen & Rohrer-Murphy, 1999, p. 62), particularly in the conception of knowledge construction emerging from interaction among humans and their contexts. Within activity theory "conscious learning emerges from activity (performance), not as a precursor to it" (p. 62).

Activity theory posits human activity as mediated by tools, both Vygotsky's model (Figure 1A) and the common reformulation (Figure 1B) include an individual or "subject" who uses a tool or tools (mediating artifacts) to achieve objectives (Engeström, 2009, p. 54; Vygotsky, 1978, p. 40).

Within activity theory "conscious learning emerges from activity (performance), not as a precursor to it" (Jonassen & Rohrer-Murphy, 1999, p. 62). Interaction between the human (subject) and the nonhuman (mediating artifact) begets knowledge construction (object).

Engeström's (2001) graphical representation of "Leont'ev explicated ... crucial difference[s] between individual action and collective activity" (p. 54) extends the original triangle beyond the individual to include social or collective aspects of an activity system (Figure 2).

In this depiction, the subject also engages in an activity, mediated by artifact and directed towards an object. This activity occurs within a context of rules, community, and division of labor. All six elements within this activity system relate to each other, and yet tensions can develop within and between the elements. The following are examples of tensions related to the CHAT elements (Engeström, 2001): (1) "*Primary contradiction* involving tensions arising anywhere within any of the CHAT elements"; (2) "*Secondary contradiction* involving tensions arising between CHAT elements"; (3) "*Tertiary contradiction* involving tensions arising between the new and the old activity system"; and (4) "*Quaternary contradiction* involving tensions arising between activity systems that may result in boundary crossings from one activity system to another" (Rückriem, 2009, p. 151).

This reconceptualization of an activity system "turned the focus on complex interrelations between the individual and his or her community" (Engeström, 2009, p. 55). Within this model, internal activities are examined alongside external activities as they transform into each other.

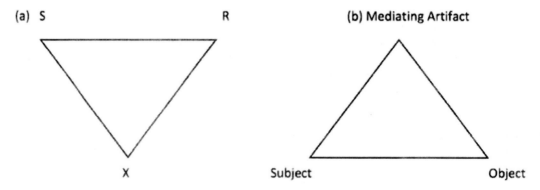

(a) S   R

X

(b) **Mediating Artifact**

Subject   Object

Source: Adapted from Engeström (1999).

FIGURE 1
Vygotsky's Model and (b) Engeström's Reformulation

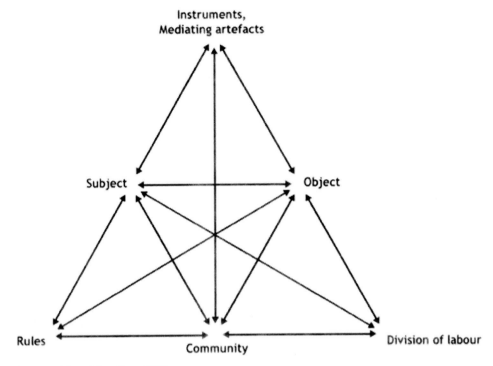

Source: Adapted from Bury (2012).

FIGURE 2
Structure of a Human Activity System as Envisioned by Engeström (2009)

In third generation activity systems, boundary crossing includes the interaction of (minimally) two interacting activity systems (Engeström, 2001). In Figure 3, boundary crossing occurs when members of two activity systems engage in a shared object (Object 2), which results in a new, potentially shared or jointly constructed object (Object 3). When boundary crossing becomes purposeful and prevalent, the jointly constructed object can become its own new activity system.

When knowledge construction is the object, boundary crossing occurs when members of Activity Systems A and B engage in a shared object, sense-making (Engeström, 2001). This results in a new, potentially shared or jointly constructed approach to solving a problem. Sense-making in this context, Object 3, can be seen as the potential for collaborative knowledge construction.

CONCEPTUALIZING LEARNING OPPORTUNITIES AS ACTIVITY SYSTEMS

For the purpose of our project, conceptualizing xMOOCs as an instance of a formal e-learning activity system and cMOOCs as an instance of informal e-learning activity provides a means by which to compare and contrast these two approaches to MOOCs.

Formal and Informal Activity Systems

Formal learning, sometimes referred to as traditional or formal education, has been defined as "(i) organized deliberately to fulfill the specific purpose of transmission, (ii) extracted from the manifold of daily life, placed in a special setting and carried out

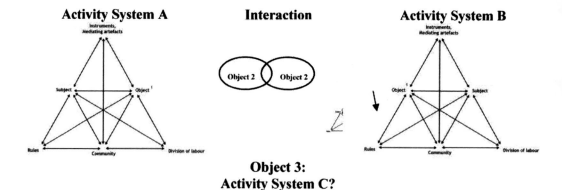

Source: Adapted from Bury (2012).

FIGURE 3
Two Interacting Activity Systems for the Third Generation Activity Theory

according to specific routines, and (iii) made the responsibility of the larger social group" (Scribner & Cole, 1973, p. 555). It can also refer to "learners in classes being taught by teachers who deliver comprehensive, multi-year curricula" (Schwier & Seaton, 2013, p. 2). Formal learning is "institutionally sponsored or highly structured, i.e., learning that happens in courses, classrooms, and schools, resulting in learners receiving grades, degrees, diplomas, and certificates" (Dabbagh & Kitsantas, 2011, p. 2).

Informal learning has been defined simply as learning done "outside any educational institutions or organized courses" (Livingstone, 2007, p. 2). Indeed, informal learning is often defined as being "the opposite of schools" (Crowley, Pierroux, & Knutson, (2014, p. 466). Its characteristics have been identified as involving (1) "incidental, learner-initiated activities ... delineated by absence of formal assessment" (Wright et al., 2013, p. 54); (2) "free choice, include a diverse and nonstandardized range of topics, and have flexible structures, socially rich interactions, and no externally imposed assessments" (Crowley et al., 2014, p. 466); or (3) "institutional, curricular, and externally imposed authority" (Wright et al., 2013, p. 54).

For Dabbagh and Kitsantas (2011) informal learning involves learning driven primarily by the learner and "happens through observation, trial and error, asking for help, conversing with others, listening to stories, reflecting on a day's events, or stimulated by general interests" (p. 12). Informal learning "can be pervasive in peer-to-peer interactions within school, and formal learning may take place in non-institutional settings such as community centers, or during an 'instructional moment' when a parent mimics didactic instruction" (Bransford et al., 2006, p. 29). The term informal learning has a negative prefix adding both a negative denotation to the term, at the same time fixing it as opposite to formal learning. Compounding the negativity, as Billet (2013) pointed out, "to describe something by what it is not (that is, informal or non-formal is seen primarily in contrast within educational institutions) is unhelpful in characterizing and appraising it effectively" (p. 131).

In Table 1, each row lists a CHAT element (left hand column). The second column, offers CHAT generalized descriptions of formal learning from the broader and xMooc literature. Information presented in the second column serves to define formal learning broadly conceptualized as an activity system. Table 1

TABLE 1
CHAT and Formal Learning

CHAT Elements	*From Broader Literature*	*From xMOOC Literature*
Subject	Learner	Learner
Object(ive)s	"Measured outcomes" (Colley, Hodkinson & Malcolm, 2003, p. 23); "specific purpose of transmission" (Scribner & Cole, 1973, p. 555); "standards of performance" (Bransford et al., 2006, p. 23)	"learning where there are clear right and wrong answers" (Ebben & Murphy, 2014, p. 336)
Mediating artifacts	"course management system (CMS)" (Garrison, 2011, p. 28)	"MOOC platforms" (Jordan, 2014, p. 134); "learning management systems" (Haber, 2014, p. 1)
Rules	"Planned and structured" (Colley, Hodkinson & Malcolm, 2003, p. 23); "planned curriculum" (Tusting, 2003, p. 6); "highly structured" (Dabbagh & Kitsantas, 2011, p. 2); "didactic instructional practices" (Bransford et al., 2006, p. 23)	"cognitivist behaviorist pedagogical design" (Ebben & Murphy, 2014, p. 335); "a more behaviorist approach" (Conole, 2014, p. 69); "lectures, reading and homework assignment, assessments, and discussions" (Haber, 2014, p. 41)
Community	"state regulated institutions" (Wright et al., 2013, p. 54) "learners in classes" (Schwier & Seaton, 2013, p. 2)	"a range of elite universities" (Jordan, 2014, p. 134) "replicating traditional classroom models" (Haber, 2014, p. 41)
Division of labor	"hierarchical" (Tusting, 2003, p. 6; Wright et al., 2013, p. 54); "taught by teachers" (Schwier & Seaton, 2013, p. 2); "teacher as authority" (Colley, Hodkinson, & Malcolm, 2003, p. 23)	"delivery of content via professors" (Conole, 2014, p. 70);

provides the means by which to conceptualize xMOOC as formal activity systems.

In Table 2, each row lists a CHAT element (left hand column). The second column offers CHAT generalized descriptions of informal learning from the literature. Information presented in the second column serves to both define informal learning as conceptualized as an activity system. In this Table 2, it provides the means by which to conceptualize cMOOCs as informal activity systems.

Conceptualizing xMOOCs and cMOOCs as "representing opposing pedagogies or ideologies … threatens to blur more interesting distinctions and overlaps between the two" (Haber, 2014, p. 40). In the following section, we examine the notion of boundary crossings in MOOCs.

Need for Boundary Crossings in MOOCs. Conole (2014) suggested learning "occurs along a spectrum from formal to informal; from loosely based resource-based learn-

ing to a structured time-defined course, which is accredited" (p. 72), whereas Hall (2009) noted that formal and informal learning should be connected to optimize learning and that learning is most effective when learners engage in both formal and informal learning activities. Boundary crossing between activity systems may lead to expansive learning activities, which "produces culturally new patterns of activity" (Engeström, 2001, p. 139), and potentially leading to a new activity system. Boundary crossing "occurs because human beings are involved in multiple activities and have to move between them" (Engeström, 2009, p. 315).

Bunderup Dohn (2009) proposed adopting pedagogical strategies that transcend discrepancies in e-learning (and/or Web 2.0) environments in order to accommodate these tensions. Such strategies would involve "boundary practice" (p. 354), an approach to learning that "borders on and to some extent incorporates

TABLE 2
CHAT and Informal Learning

CHAT Elements	From Broader Literature	From cMOOC Literature
Subject	Learner	Learner
Object(ive)s	"Outcomes imprecise/unmeasurable" (Colley, Hodkinson, & Malcolm, 2003; p. 23); "incidental learning" (Tusting, 2003, p. 5)	"unpremeditated" (Tusting, 2003, p. 5); "no pre-defined expectations" (McAuley et al., 2010, p. 4); "independent study" (Hall, 2009, p. 31)
Mediating artifact	"online social network" (McAuley et al., 2010, p. 4); "mobile devices, applications, and social networking technologies" (Wright, Short, & Parchoma, 2013, p. 55)	"Twitter, blogs, wikis" (Conole, 2014, p. 70); software tools for discovery, connection, and co-creation" (Milligan et al., 2013, p. 150)
Rules	"Organic and evolving" (Colley, Hodkinson, & Malcolm, 2003; p. 23); "unorganized, unsystematic, and regularly serendipitous" (Schwier & Seaton, 2013, p. 2); "non-course-based" (Tusting, 2003, p. 7)	"connectivist pedagogy" (Conole, 2014, p. 69); "connectivist framework" (Haber, 2014, p. 38); "flexible content" (Ebben & Murphy, 2014, p. 334)
Community	"noneducational settings" (Malcolm et al., 2003, p. 314) "outside any educational institutions or organized courses" (Livingstone, 2007, p. 2) "people from a range of sectors" (Tusting, 2003, p. 7) "others" (Dabbagh & Kitsantas, 2011, p. 12)	"distributed network of peers" (Conole, 2014, p. 70); "networked learners" (Haber, 2014, p. 38); "active participants, lurkers" (Milligan et al., 2013, p. 156); "facilitators" (McAuley et al., 2010, p. 6)
Division of labor	"learner-centered, negotiated pedagogy" (Colley et al., 2003, p. 23); "no teacher involved" (Colley et al., 2003, p. 23) "self-directedness" (Schwier & Seaton, 2013, p. 1); "learner-initiated" (Wright et al., 2013, p. 55)	"controlled by the learners" (Milligan et al., 2013, para. 4); "learning through peers" (Conole, 2014, p. 70; "self-organize" (McAuley et al., 2010, p. 4); "self-regulation" (Milligan et al., 2013, p. 157)

the practices of" both working life and educational settings (p. 354). The development of a MOOC, specially designed to include opportunities for both formal and informal learning, is positioned as a form of boundary crossing object, where the intent is to have learners engage with interrelated "attributes of formality and informality" (Wright et al., 2013, p. 55).

HYBRID MOOC DESIGN

Our project involved a design of a MOOC inspired by *The Frankenstein Bicentennial Project* (Arizona State University, 2014). In April 2014, one member of our research team was invited to join other scholars, educators, artists, and writers for a 3-day symposium hosted by Arizona State University. She was part of a subgroup of eight whose interests and

experiences best aligned with the subtheme "MOOCenstein: Frankenstein Goes Global":

> The MOOC will use the novel, *Frankenstein*, as a gateway for connecting STEM content with humanities, social sciences and arts, and it is designed to create an international community of thinkers critically engaged with the ethical, legal and societal issues raised by Frankenstein beyond traditional college and university environments. (Arizona State University, 2014, para. 6)

Inspired by this goal and the working group, this member of our research team designed *From Frankenstein to Post-Humanism*. A key principle for the hybrid MOOC design was that it would be inclusive of learning opportunities arising from both formal dimensions (instructor-designed tasks) and informal dimensions (emergent, autonomous and collective, participant activities). The aim of the design was to encourage thought-provoking investigation, discussion, and ideas around the central concepts of the novel *Frankenstein* and posthumanism. Key activities included exploring ideas and themes raised in Mary Shelley's *Frankenstein*, engaging in critical thinking and discussion within an international community that included opportunities to form subcommunities of individuals with shared research interests, and creating or curating artifacts, and showcasing a portfolio of accomplishments. The MOOC design functioned as the locus for our study.

THE STUDY

Our case study was temporally situated within the design stage of MOOC course creation. The inquiry was guided by the question of how instructional designers perceived future learners' opportunities for boundary crossing between formal and informal learning within the *Frankenstein to Post-Humanism* MOOC design.

The population was postsecondary level instructional designers. The sampling frame included those involved in instructional design (practitioners or academics) who had a minimum of 5 years' experience, particularly in relation to e-learning in Canadian or U.S. universities. Prospective participants were selected from blogs and websites (some of which list instructional design, teaching and learning centers, and similar departments within institutions). Academic and conference papers were also used as sources. The result was a convenience sample of eight instructional designers. To retain anonymity, each participant was identified by the acronym ID and a randomly assigned number from 1 to 8 (ID1, ID2, ID3, and so on).

The "exploratory sequential" (Creswell, 2012, p. 541) research design for the case study involved three phases. Beginning with survey data and its analysis led to the development of questions for the semistructured focus group interviews with seven of the eight research participants who were divided into two focus groups. Focus group interviews were conducted for the purpose of gaining insight into participants' approaches to analyzing the learning design in the MOOC. The focus group findings were then analyzed to develop the semistructured protocol for individual interviews. A semistructured interview process was used to allow the flexibility to pursue emergent ideas.

Phase I: Online Survey

The online survey involved participants completing a 45-question 4-point Likert style survey. The questions related to opportunities for formal and informal learning in the *From Frankenstein to Post-Humanism* MOOC design. Fifteen core questions were asked about each of three sections within the course design (introductory, core, and end). Engeström's (2009) third generation of cultural historical activity theory (CHAT) informed the survey design. Survey questions were created to align with CHAT-elements, as illustrated in Table 3.

Participants were asked to examine the course design and then to complete the survey. The survey provided quantitative data and also functioned as a method of comprehensive introduction to the course design itself. It was orientation to key concepts explored.

Phase II: Focus Group Interviews

Once the surveys had been completed, research participants were invited to participate in a semi-structured focus group interview to provide more detailed information about their perceptions of opportunities for learners to engage in formal and informal learning opportunities. The focus group interviews included questions of how the participants would define formal and informal learning, and how they saw opportunities for formal or informal learning experiences in the MOOC design. Through the interview, opportunities for boundary crossing between formal and

TABLE 3
CHAT Elements and Related Questions

Object(ive)	Why is the activity taking place?
Mediating artifact	What means are involved in performing the activity?
Rules	What are the cultural norms, rules, and regulations governing the performance of the activity?
Division of labor	Who is responsible for what? How are they organized?
Community	What is the environment in which this activity is being carried out?

Source: Adapted from Mwanza and Engeström (2005, p. 459).

informal activity systems were explored. Data from the surveys were used to inform the creation of focus group interview questions. The following are examples of questions asked.

Phase III: Individual Interviews

The creation of individual interview questions followed a semistructured protocol based on Phase II data. A semistructured strategy allowed for exploration of key areas that emerged from the focus group data. The first question was designed to elicit responses related to the CHAT elements *subject* and *community*; the second question to the CHAT element *object(ive)s*; the third question *rules*; the fourth *mediating artifacts*; and the fifth *division of labor*. Included with the questions were selected quotations from the focus group transcripts that were particularly interesting, puzzling, or salient. For example, ID5 "So to a certain extent, even informal learning you have to design into your course." Each participant was asked to comment further on selected quotations.

Data Analysis

The data were reported in a table that provided a comprehensive image of participant responses question by question. In order to undertake more refined observations, a method of scoring the data were used that involved the creation of codes. The codes (derived from CHAT elements and instances of formal and informal learning opportunities, as well as opportunities for boundary crossing) were then directly applied to the list of survey questions. In addition, summed scores based on the number of participants who selected each measure on a Likert style scale (strongly agree, agree, disagree, strongly disagree) were calculated. Along with this coding, cross tabulations were conducted to identify interdependent relationships between formal and informal learning opportunities, as well as between formal and informal CHAT elements. This information allowed us to "summarize the overall trends or tendencies" from the survey data (Creswell, 2012, p. 183).

A constant comparative method of analysis was used to examine the focus group and individual interview data sets (Creswell, 2012, p. 434), thereby identifying emergent themes arising from participants' extrapolations of the survey data. Phases II and III data analysis involved examining tensions and contradictions between formal and informal learning opportunities in order to consider insights into participants' perceptions of learners' opportunities for boundary crossing. For example with the CHAT element *rules*, results were interpreted by identifying areas of contradiction or tension—specifically, "open" versus "structured" and "possibilities" versus "objectives." This could underlie tensions and/or contradictions between formal and informal learning activity systems identified in the survey results. Tensions and/or contradictions within an activity system can lead to boundary crossing between activity systems. Corroboration of evidence across data sets were needed to garner a clearer understanding of the boundary-crossing potential within the MOOC design.

DISCUSSION OF THE FINDINGS

Formal and Informal Learning as Activity Systems

Fundamental to answering the first two sub-questions was the establishment of formal and informal learning as activity systems. The notion of formal and informal learning conceived as activity systems was presented in the literature review, with xMOOCs and cMOOCs operating as examples of formal and informal e-learning, respectively. Research findings upheld this conception of formal and informal learning as activity systems. Interpretation of the reported findings in order to answer our research questions began with charting formal and informal learning activity systems. This charting allowed for close examination and comparison of research findings to the literature.

In addition to the charts, research results related to the five themes (1, lost and found; 2, purpose and potential; 3, triggers and barriers, 4, individual in community; and 5, direction and self-directed). Through examination of the themes, quaternary tensions (between activity systems) provided insights and answers related to participant perceptions of learners' opportunities for boundary crossing between formal and informal learning within the MOOC design. Results from the research data related to the CHAT elements extended examination and analysis of the participants' perceptions of opportunities for formal and informal learning activities in the MOOC design to include perceptions of boundary crossing.

Building upon Table 1, from the data a fourth column was added that represents participants' definitions of formal learning as drawn from the data (refer to Table 4). Each row in Table 4 demonstrates how the findings confirmed what was evident in the literature, and where they differed. Differences were interpreted to arise from the influence of the

three distinct formal learning contexts compared in Table 4. For example, the row for *rules*, behaviorist/cognitivist theories of learning and xMOOCs was not indicated in the findings. This could be interpreted that how MOOCs "may vary in pedagogical underpinnings" (Ebben & Murphy, 2014, p. 335) is more often an aspect of xMOOC literature. Another likely context related difference was the participant perception of "payment associated."

Similarities between the finding and the literature were also identified by scanning across the rows, again for example the CHAT element *rules*. Generalized descriptors of formal learning *rules* from the second column (planned and structured, planned curriculum, highly structured, and didactic instructional practices) run parallel to participant perceptions of *rules* from the fourth column (traditionally designed, systematic and structured, and structured learning path). As a result of such similarities across the rows, an overarching description can be derived. A formal e-learning activity system involves predefined outcomes, and structured learning tasks, potentially influenced by behavioralist/cognitivist theories of learning, wherein specific learning management systems (LMS) influence primarily teacher driven interactions between teachers and students.

Similarly, drawing from Table 2 by adding a fourth column, Table 5 presents participants' definitions of informal learning as drawn from the data. The table allows for easy access to compare and contrast the findings. That is, similarities in the descriptors could be seen across almost all the rows. For example, the similarities between the descriptors in the row *mediating artifact*, wherein the tools used in e-learning such as MOOCs "encompass all forms of media—from text, to video, from sound recordings to immersive worlds" (Anderson & Kanuka, 2003, para. 11) are evident.

As a result of similarities in the descriptors identified across all columns and rows, an overarching description emerged. An informal

TABLE 4
CHAT and Formal Learning

CHAT Elements	From Broad Literature	From xMOOC Literature	Research Participant Perceptions
Subject	Learner	Learner	(Hypothetical) Learner
Object(ive)s	"Measured outcomes" (Colley et al., 2003, p. 23); "specific purpose of transmission" (Scribner & Cole, 1973, p. 555); "standards of performance" (Bransford et al., 2006, p. 23)	"learning where there are clear right and wrong answers" (Ebben & Murphy, 2014, p. 336)	Purpose (ID6), goals (ID7), a certain outcome (ID6), defined outcomes … goal or end (ID4), explicit learning objectives (ID1), intentional learning (ID5)
Mediating artifacts	"course management system (CMS)" (Garrison, 2011, p. 28)	"MOOC platforms" (Jordan, 2014, p. 134); "learning management systems" (Haber, 2014, p. 1)	course outline (ID2), assignments (ID7), LMS (ID6), Blackboard (ID2; ID4), discussion forums (ID7), discussion boards and wikis (ID3)
Rules	"Planned and structured" (Colley et al., 2003, p. 23); "planned curriculum" (Tusting, 2003, p. 6); "highly structured" (Dabbagh & Kitsantas, 2011, p. 2); "didactic instructional practices" (Bransford et al., 2006, p. 23)	"cognitivist behaviorist pedagogical design" (Ebben & Murphy, 2014, p. 335); "a more behaviorist approach" (Conole, 2014, p. 69); "lectures, reading and homework assignment, assessments, and discussions" (Haber, 2014, p. 41)	payment associated (ID3), traditionally designed (ID1), instructions (ID4), rigid (ID5), less deviation (ID7), systematic and … structured (ID5) structured learning path (ID4), step-by-step activities (ID2)
Community	"state regulated institutions" (Wright et al., 2013, p. 54) "learners in classes" (Schwier & Seaton, 2013, p. 2)	"a range of elite universities" (Jordan, 2014, p. 34) "replicating traditional classroom models" (Haber, 2014, p. 41)	Students (ID1; ID2), trained professionals (ID1)
Division of labor	"hierarchical" (Tusting, 2003, p. 6; Wright et al., 2013, p. 54); "taught by teachers" (Schwier & Seaton, 2013, p. 2); "teacher as authority" (Colley et al., 2003, p. 23)	"delivery of content via professors" (Conole, 2014, p. 70)	Central teacher … professor or instructor (ID3), facilitated (ID7), delivered (ID1)

e-learning activity system involves Web 2.0 tools, particularly social media, to achieve unknown or unknowable learning outcomes. This is often aligned with connectivist theory of learning and potentially involving a wide range of people, including life-long learners, peers, and lurkers.

Differences also became apparent from scanning the rows in Table 5. For example, with the CHAT element *community,* the generalized informal learning descriptors that descriptors from the literature (column two), and cMOOC descriptors (column three) differ from participant descriptors. The same row of column four offers cMOOC-related descriptors: learners, peers, instructor(s), connections with others via social media, and potentially including external experts. The far right or fourth column of the same row provides participant descriptors for informal *community* in a MOOC design: lifelong-learners and peers. Research participant perceptions of informal learning support the notion of informal learning as an activity system.

Moving from mapping CHAT element, in Tables 4 and 5, consideration of specific

TABLE 5
CHAT and Informal Learning

CHAT Elements	From Broad Literature	From cMOOC Literature	Research Participant Perspectives
Subject	Learner	Learner	(Hypothetical) learner
Object(ive)s	"Outcomes imprecise/unmeasurable" (Colley et al., 2003; p. 23); "incidental learning" (Tusting, 2003, p. 5)	"unpremeditated" (Tusting, 2003, p. 5); "no predefined expectations" (McAuley et al., 2010, p. 4); "independent study" (Hall, 2009, p. 31)	not an intended learning outcome or product (ID6), anything (ID4), accidental (ID2), tangents (ID4)
Mediating artifacts	"online social network" (McAuley et al., 2010, p. 4); "mobile devices, applications, and social networking technologies" (Wright, Short, & Parchoma, 2013, p. 55);	"Twitter, blogs, wikis" (Conole, 2014, p. 70); software tools for discovery, connection, and co-creation" (Milligan et al., 2013, p. 150)	Google Hangouts (ID1), YouTube, Blogs (ID5), Facebook, Twitter (ID2, ID7), discussion forums (ID7)
Rules	"Organic and evolving" (Colley et al., 2003; p. 23); "unorganized, unsystematic, and regularly serendipitous" (Schwier & Seaton, 2013, p. 2); "non-course-based" (Tusting, 2003, p. 7)	"connectivist pedagogy" (Conole, 2014, p. 69); "connectivist framework" (Haber, 2014, p. 38); "flexible content" (Ebben & Murphy, 2014, p. 334)	connectivism (ID3), very unstructured (ID5), aren't instructions (ID3), choices (ID6; ID7), not packaged (ID6), flexibility (ID6), ad hoc, opportunity, no limitation (ID4)
Community	"noneducational settings" (Malcolm et al., 2003, p. 314) "outside any educational institutions or organized courses" (Livingstone, 2007, p. 2) "people from a range of sectors" (Tusting, 2003, p. 7) "others" (Dabbagh & Kitsantas, 2011, p. 12)	"distributed network of peers" (Conole, 2014, p. 70); "networked learners" (Haber, 2014, p. 38); "active participants, lurkers" (Milligan et al., 2013, p. 156); "facilitators" (McAuley et al., 2010, p. 6)	lifelong-learners (ID6), peers
Division of labor	"Learner-centered, negotiated pedagogy" (Colley et al., 2003, p. 23); "no teacher involved" (Colley et al., (2003, p. 23) "self-directedness" (Schwier & Seaton, 2013, p. 1); "learner-initiated" (Wright et al., 2013, p. 55)	"controlled by the learners" (Milligan, et al., 2013, para. 4); "learning through peers" (Conole, 2014, p. 70; "self-organize" (McAuley et al., 2010, p. 4); "self-regulation" (Milligan, et al., 2013, p. 157)	Not facilitated (ID7), learn from each other, peer guidance (ID7), self-directed (ID3; ID4; ID7) self-motivated (ID2)

CHAT elements related to the five themes: (1) lost and found; (2) purpose and potential; (3) triggers and barriers; (4) individual in community; and (5) direction and self-directed.

First, the theme *lost and found* recognized a tension between formal learning CHAT element *rules* as a means of establishing and maintaining structure versus perceptions of unstructured informal learning. Quaternary tensions could also be seen in relation to the CHAT element *object(ive)s*. This was specifically found between formal learning where objectives are typically preestablished, whereas informal learning objectives may yet to be determined, if ever. Both of these themes and their related findings proved also to be corroborated by the literature.

Second, in relation to the theme *individual in community*, tensions and contradictions in relation to the CHAT element *community* proved emergent and thus difficult to perceive in a MOOC design. An interpretation of the emergent nature of community, therefore not likely visible in a MOOC design, was supported by the literature. The literature also supported observation of tensions identified in relation to both formal and informal learning *mediating artifacts* as potentially both supportive and inhibiting learning in the MOOC design.

Third, findings in relation to the theme *triggers and barriers* demonstrated participants perceived a greater number of instances of opportunities for formal learning within the *mediating artifacts* in the MOOC design. The literature supported observation of tensions identified in relation to both formal and informal learning *mediating artifacts* as potentially both supportive and inhibiting learning in the MOOC design.

Fourth, the theme *purpose and potential* indicated the objective(s) CHAT element was perceived by research participants as derived from learner need or preference, whether learning *object(ive)s* are predefined in a formal learning context, or possibilities available in an informal learning context. If the object of each activity system is learning, the outcome of the object will vary between the systems.

Fifth, the CHAT element *division of labor* related to tensions between teacher and self-direction in formal learning also pointed to quaternary tensions between formal learning teacher direction and informal learning self-direction. Within the perception of formal and informal learning in MOOCs, learner self-direction or self-motivation (as indicated in Table 4 and 5) played a key role. "Any particular learner or group of learners may manifest elements of self-directedness in their learning whether it be within a formal ... or informal learning" (Schwier & Seaton, 2013, p. 2).

Examination of participant definitions of formal and informal learning in the literature and the data answered our research questions in part and allowed for an interpretation supportive of the notion of formal and informal learning conceived as activity systems. Interestingly, another finding emerged from this study, supported by the literature, indicated that while formal learning was identified for what it is, informal learning was identified for what it is not.

INSIGHTS DRAWN FROM THE DATA

Participants' conceptions of formal and informal learning influenced their perceptions of opportunities for boundary crossing in a MOOC design. Examination of participant definitions of both formal and informal learning in the literature and from the data allowed for an interpretation supportive of the notion of formal and informal learning conceived as activity systems. Further, while formal learning was identified for what it is, informal learning was identified for what it is not. Overall, findings in this study were supported by the literature.

Formal and Informal Learning. Findings were investigated to identify participants' perceptions of opportunities for formal and informal learning in the MOOC design (e.g., with the conceptualization of these learning contexts as activity systems). The use of negative wording (predominantly via prefixes such as un- and in-) to describe informal learning as not or opposite to formal learning particularly highlighted the participants' perceptions of formal and informal learning as distinct activity systems. A conclusion to be drawn was that as the sample of designers who participated in the study work within formal learning environments, it is plausible participants' professional experience was in a context where informal learning design was less likely to occur. Findings were examined to reveal interpretation such as the possibility of informal learning residing outside the professional scope of participants, and not typically be included in their instructional design thinking or practice.

Boundary Crossing. Findings supportive of formal and informal learning as activity systems allowed for examination of boundary crossing between these two systems (Engeström, 2001). Conclusions can be drawn in relation to each of the five major findings from this study.

First, a finding of our research was that participants in the study perceived that formal rules (as instantiated in course outlines, schedules, or assignments) as offering guidance to future learners for both formal and informal learning opportunities in the MOOC design. Formal rules would show future learners how to navigate content, assignments, and so on, therein providing a learning pathway or guide by which a learner could navigate a course. A conclusion to be drawn from this finding is that participants, as instructional designers in higher education contexts, placed primary importance on structure and guidance in course design. Instructional designers, such as the participants in this study, function within formal learning academic environments with numerous structures, systems, approaches, and procedures. It can also be concluded that informal learning rules may guide future learners' social behavior (e.g., netiquette), even though this guidance is not directly intended to support learners through the achievement of learning goals. These two sets of formal and informal rules can be seen as setting a stage for a potential primary tension (Rückriem, 2009) arising within the CHAT element rules.

A second finding was that mediating artifacts or tools, particularly online technologies, can be supportive of, or prohibitive to, learning. Participants' perceived technology in the MOOC design as involving in how learners interact with activities, resources, as well as with each other. Given that the design provided opportunities for future learners to use a varied range of tools, individual choices of mediating artifacts opened possibilities for secondary tensions (Rückriem, 2009) as a result between the CHAT elements of mediating artifacts and community continuity.

A third finding was that of participants' perception of objectives in formal learning as known and knowable, and informal learning as unknown, possibly unknowable. This finding can be seen to align with Goodyear, Carvalho, and Bonderup Dohn's (2014) questioning of "whether it is actually possible to design for someone else's learning" (p. 139). What can be gleaned from this contradiction is that in the absence of formal learning objectives, informal learning perhaps could be seen to serve as

a catalyst for an array of learning. Through informal learning, future learners will have the opportunities to seek information, test ideas, and develop new understanding through their own decisions and actions. Therefore, if we, like the participants in this study, consider the formal learning activity system as the benchmark activity system, then interactions with the informal, unknowable activity system are likely to result in tertiary contractions (Rückriem, 2009) between systems.

A fourth finding involved participants' perception of self-direction as a factor in both formal and informal learning. What can be taken from this is that learners online, such as in a MOOC, take on a variety of roles and responsibilities. In other words, learners in online courses are primarily responsible for the task of directing their own learning. Therefore, the CHAT element of division of labor cannot be predicted, but will likely lead to boundary crossings, as a response to quaternary contradictions (Rückriem, 2009) among varied formal and informal roles and responsibilities.

The fifth finding demonstrated how participants did not perceive the potential for community in the MOOC design. Research participants' experience with the MOOC, housed in a learning management system (LMS), occurred in the design stage. In other words the participants' experienced the MOOC on their own. What can be concluded is that a community is emergent in a MOOC and it would be more apparent during or post implementation.

Summary. Participants' perceptions of the MOOC design were mapped against CHAT elements. Figure 4 presents Object 1-learners with the general objective of engaging in formal learning, and Object 2-learners with the general objective of informal learning. Allowing for boundary crossing between these activity systems, Object 3 thus moves to a "potentially shared or jointly constructed object" (Engeström, 2001, p. 136).

From the conceptualization of boundary crossing in Figure 4, it is possible to conclude the possibility of not only mapping formal and

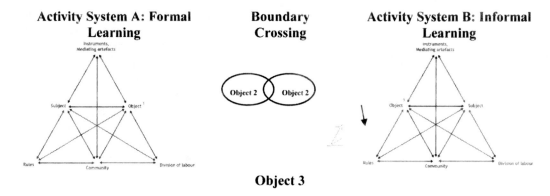

| Activity System A: Formal Learning | Boundary Crossing | Activity System B: Informal Learning |

Object 3

Activity System 3: Designed opportunities for boundary crossing between formal and informal learning activity systems provides opportunites for future students to undertake collaborative, interdisciplinary sense-making activities, resulting in a new activity system.

Source: Adapted from Bury (2012).

FIGURE 4
Interacting Formal and Informal Activity Systems Resulting in an Emergent MOOC Activity System

informal learning, but also to map a new conceptualization of an activity system, specifically a MOOC activity system that arises from the tensions identified between formal and informal learning activity systems.

CONCLUSIONS AND IMPLICATIONS

Our study provides evidence that designs for formal and informal learning opportunities can be conceptualized as separate but potentially interacting activity systems. The use of CHAT elements to analyze data collected from professional instructional designers' perspectives on one MOOC design—which includes opportunities for both formal and informal learning activities—identifies potential primary, secondary, tertiary, and quaternary tensions and contradictions indicated that inclusion of both formal and informal learning activities within a single MOOC design that are likely to result in: (a) at least, the potential for future learners' to cross boundaries between formal and informal activity systems and (b) even more likely, result in the emergence of a new, MOOC-specific activity system. These insights can

inform both future research approaches to examining what happens in MOOCs and practitioner considerations for future MOOC designs.

REFERENCES

Anders, A. (2015). Theories and applications of massive open online courses (MOOCs): The case for hybrid design. *International Review of Research in Open and Distance Learning, 16*(6), 39–61.

Arizona State University. (2014). The Frankenstein bicentennial project [Website]. *Center for Science and the Imagination.* Retrieved from http://csi.asu.edu/category/projects/frankenstein-bicentennial/

Anderson, T., & Kanuka, H. (2003). *e-Research.* Boston, MA: Allyn and Bacon.

Barsalou, L. W., Breazeal, C., & Smith, L. (2007). Cognition as coordinated non-cognition. *Cognitive Processing, 8*(2), 79–91.

Billet, S. (2013). Learning through practice: Beyond informal and towards a framework for learning through practice. In *Revisiting Global Trends in TVET: Reflections on theory and practice* (pp. 123–163). Bonn, Germany: UNESCO.

Bonderup Dohn, N. (2009). Web 2.0: Inherent tensions and evident challenges for education. *International Journal of Computer Supported Collaborative Learning, 4*(3), 343–363.

Bransford, J. D, Barron, B., Pea, R. D., Meltzoff, A., Kuhl, P., Bell, P., … Sabelli, N.H. (2006). Foundations and opportunities for an interdisciplinary science of learning. In R. K. Sawyer (Ed.) *The Learning Sciences* (pp. 19–34). Cambridge, England: Cambridge University Press.

Bury, M. (2012). Activity system [Digital image]. Retrieved from Wikimedia Commons Website: https://commons.wikimedia.org/wiki/File:Activity_system.png

Colley, H., Hodkinson, P., & Malcolm, J. (2003) *Non-formal learning: Mapping the conceptual terrain. A consultation report.* Leeds, England: University of Leeds Lifelong Learning Institute. Retrieved from http://www.infed.org/archives/e-texts/colley_informal_learning.htm

Conole, G. (2014). A new classification schema for MOOCs. *The International Journal for Innovation and Quality in Learning,* 65–77. Retrieved from http://cdn.efquel.org/wp-content/blogs.dir/6/files/2013/02/INNOQUAL-Issue-3-Publication-Sep-2014-FINAL-w-cover.pdf#page=72

Creswell, J. W. (2012). *Educational research.* Boston, MA: Pearson.

Crotty, M. (2010). *The foundations of social research.* London, England: SAGE.

Crowley, K., Pierroux, P., & Knutson, K. (2014). Informal learning in museums. In R. K. Sawyer (Ed.) *The learning sciences* (2nd ed., pp. 19–34). Cambridge, England: Cambridge University Press.

Dabbagh, N., & Kitsantas, A. (2011). PLE, social media, and self-regulated learning: A natural formula for connection formal and informal learning. *The Internet and Higher Education, 5*(1). Retrieved from http://www.sciencedirect.com/science/journal/10967516/15/1

Downes, S. (2017). New models of open and distance learning. In M. Jemni, KINSHUK, & M. Khribi (Eds.), *New models of open and distance learning in open education: From OERs to MOOCs* (pp.1–22). Berlin, Germany: Springer.

Ebben, M., & Murphy, J. S. (2014). Unpacking MOOC scholarly discourse: A review of nascent MOOC scholarship. *Learning, Media and Technology, 39*(3), 328–345.

Engeström, Y. (2001). Expansive learning at work: Toward an activity theoretical reconceptualization. *Journal of Education at Work, 14*(1), 133–156.

Engeström, Y. (2009). Expansive learning: Towards an activity-theoretical reconceptualization. In K. Illeris (Ed.), *Contemporary theories of learning* (pp. 53–73). New York, NY: Routledge.

Garrison, R. D. (2011). *E-learning in the 21st century.* New York, NY: Routledge.

Goodyear, P., Carvalho, L., & Bunderup Dohn, N. (2014). Design for networked learning: Framing relations between participants' activities and the physical setting. In S. Bayne, C. Jones, M. de Laat, T. Ryberg, & C. Sinclair, *Proceedings of the 9th International Conference of Networked Learning* (pp. 137–144). Retrieved from http://www.lancaster.ac.uk/fss/organisations/netlc/past/nlc2014/abstracts/pdf/goodyear.pdf

Haber, J. (2014). *MOOCs.* Cambridge, MA: MIT Press.

Hall, R. (2009). Towards a fusion of formal and informal learning environments: The impact of the read/write web. *Electronic Journal of e-Learning, 7*(1), 29–40.

Johnson, L., Adams Becker, S., Cummins, M., Estrada, V., Freeman, A., & Ludgate, H. (2013). *NMC Horizon Report: 2013 Higher Education Edition.* Austin, TX: New Media Consortium.

Jonassen, D. H., & Roher-Murphy, L. (1999). Activity theory as framework for designing constructivist learning environments. *Educational Technology Research and Development, 47*(1), 61–79.

Jordan, K. (2014). Initial trends in enrolment and completion of massive open online courses. *The International Review of Research in Open and Distance Learning, 15*(1), 133–159.

Karagiaorgi, Y., & Symeou, L. (2005). Translating constructivism into instructional design: Potential and limitations. *Educational Technology and Society, 8*(1), 17–27.

Kowch, E. (2004). Designing effective instruction [Peer commentary on the book *Designing effective instruction,* by G. R. Morrison, S. M. Ross, & J. E. Kemp]. *Educational Technology Research and Development, 52*(4), 85–90.

Littlejohn, A. (2013). EdTech notes: Understanding massive open online courses. *CEMCA.* Retrieved from http://cemca.org.in/ckfinder/userfiles/files/EdTech%20Notes%202_Littlejohn_final_1June2013.pdf

Livingstone, D. W. (2007). Re-exploring the icebergs of adult learning: Comparative findings of the 1998 and 2004 Canadian surveys of formal and informal learning practices. *The Canadian Journal for the Study of Adult Education, 1*(24). Retrieved from http://cjsae.library.dal.ca/index.php/cjsae/article/view/1104

Malcolm, J., Hodkinson, P., & Colley, H. (2003). The interrelationships between informal and formal learning. *Journal of Workplace Learning, 15*(7/8), 313–318.

Markauskaite, L., & Goodyear, P. (2017). *Epistemic fluency and professional education: Innovation, knowledgeable action, and actionalable knowledge.* Dordrecht, The Netherlands: Springer.

McAuley, A., Stewart, B., Siemens, G., & Cormier, D. (2010*). The MOOC model for digital practice* (Report). Prince Edward Island, Canada: University of Prince Edward Island, Social Sciences and Humanities Research. Retrieved from https://oerknowledgecloud.org/sites/oerknowledgecloud.org/files/MOOC_Final_0.pdf

Milligan, C., Littlejohn, A., & Margaryan, A. (2013). Patterns of engagement in connectivist MOOCs. *Journal of Online Learning and Teaching, 9*(24). Retrieved from http://jolt.merlot.org/vol9no2/milligan_0613.htm

Mwanza, D., & Engeström, Y. (2005). Managing content in e-learning environments. *British Journal of Educational Technology, 36*(3), 453–463.

O'Toole, R. (2013*) Pedagogical strategies and technologies for peer assessment in massively open online courses (MOOCs)* ([Unpublished manuscript). University of Warwick, Coventry, England. Retrieved from http://wrap.warwick.ac.uk/54602/

Parchoma, G. (in press). Traces of cognition as a distributed phenomenon in networked learning. In N. Bonderup Dohn, S. Cramer, J.-A. Sime, M. de Laat, & T. Ryberg (Eds.), *Networked learning.* New York, NY: Springer.

Rückriem, G. (2009). Digital technology and mediation: A challenge to activity theory. In A. Sannino, H. Daniels, & K. D. Gutierrez (Eds.), *Learning and expanding with activity theory* (pp.

88–111). Cambridge, England: Cambridge University Press.

Ryberg, T., Buus, L., & Georgsen, M. (2012). Differences in understandings of networked learning theory: Connectivity or collaboration. In, L. Dirckinck-Homfeld, V. Hodgson, & D. McConnell (Eds.) *Exploring the theory, pedagogy, and practice of networked learning* (pp. 43–60). New York, NY: Springer.

Scribner, S., & Cole, M. (1973). Cognitive consequences of formal and informal learning. *Science, 182*(4112), 553–559. Retrieved from http://science.sciencemag.org/content/182/4112/553

Schwier, R. A., & Seaton, J. X. (2013). A comparison of participation patterns in selected formal, non-formal, and informal learning environments. *Canadian Journal of Learning and Technology, 39*(1), 1–15. Retrieved from http://cjlt.csj.ualberta.ca/index.php/cjlt/article/view/709

Selwyn, N., & Simons, H. (2009). Evolution and concept of case study research. In H. Simons (Ed.), *Case study research in practice* (pp. 12–28). London, England: SAGE.

Siemens, G. (2005, April 5). Connectivism: A learning theory for a digital age [Web log page]. Retrieved from http://www.elearnspace.org/Articles/connectivism.htm

Skinner, B. F. (1938). *The behaviour of organisms: An experimental analysis.* New York, NY: Appleton-Century.

Tusting, K. (2003). A review of theories of informal learning (Literacy Research Centre Working Paper No. 2). Lancaster, England: Lancaster University.

Vygotsky, L. S. (1978). *Mind in society.* Cambridge, MA: Harvard University Press.

Wright, S., Short, B., & Parchoma, G. (2013). Supporting creativity in craft brewing: A case study in iPhone use in the transition from novice towards mastery. *International Journal of Mobile and Blended Learning, 5*(3), 52–67.

THE EFFECT OF MODALITY CHANGE ON COURSE EVALUATIONS IN A STATISTICS COURSE

Vicki Ingalls
Tiffin University

The purpose of course evaluations is to allow students the opportunity to evaluate the course and the instructor. As a reflective teacher, I take the 20 years' worth of comments and numerical ratings on traditional, seated course evaluations to heart. When compared to newer evaluations from the online environment, a dichotomy exists. The purpose of the study is to explore why the evaluations are so different and to identify possible solutions to unify to chasm between seated and online perceptions to the same statistics course.

As a reflective teacher, I take the comments and numerical ratings of my course evaluations to heart. It is necessary to think long and hard about the Likert scale rankings and the constructive comments that students provide and make the necessary changes the next time the course is taught. However, I have recently found myself in a state of cognitive dissonance with respect to the student ratings in the seated versus the online environment.

The purpose of course evaluations is to allow students the opportunity to evaluate the course and the instructor. Research has been done on student evaluations with respect to student satisfaction criteria (Kirk & Spector, 2009; Rothman, Romeo, Brennan, & Mitchell, 2011), comparisons of full-time and adjuncts

(Kirk & Spector, 2009; Mueller, Mandernach, & Sanderson, 2013), and quantitative course evaluations (Constand & Pace, 2014; Royal & Stockdale, 2015) among many other facets of course evaluation. Of particular interest and relevance to this study is the student perception of synchronous versus asynchronous online education models (Offir, Lev, & Bezalel, 2008; Parenti, 2013) and the direct application to evaluation systems (Allen, Bourhis, Burrell, & Mabry, 2002; Baker, 2010; Lyke & Frank, 2012; Rothman et al., 2011; Swan, 2002).

One particular type of course evaluation, and specifically employed at the university of study, is called the IDEA student ratings inventory. The instrument is powered by Cam-

• **Vicki Ingalls**, Associate Professor of Mathematics, Tiffin University, Tiffin, OH. E-mail: ingallsv@tiffin.edu

The Quarterly Review of Distance Education, Volume 18(2), 2017, pp. 51–55
ISSN 1528-3518

pus Labs for ease of student use in its interactive online platform. The system controls for extraneous circumstances (e.g., class size, student motivation), and provides comparative scores (IDEA, n.d.). This type of course evaluation is different than many homemade evaluation instruments in that it is not just the proverbial faculty popularity contest. It is a standardized system for all universities which also allows for converted ratings compared at both the institutional and content discipline levels, including customized reports with system feedback on strengths and areas of improvement. Similar to many other evaluation instruments, it measures the summary of excellent teacher and excellent course. However, our institution chose the normative system as it also measures students' perceptions of their progress on relevant objectives, therefore attempting to measure the student learning captured the course. Our university has opted to use this same system of evaluation across both seated and online environments, as directed by Berge and Meyers (2000) and Clark (1989).

In teaching math in the seated environment at the same school for the last 20 years, I have found very positive evaluations of my courses, teaching pedagogy, and student progress on meeting the learning objectives. Because of the identical nature of IDEA evaluations across modality and a fairly newfound interest in teaching online, I found some interesting descriptive statistics in the comparison of teaching evaluations differed only by modality (i.e., same course, content, assignments, etc.). Using a Likert scale with low = 1 and high = 5, my 3-year average for seated coursework ratings was 4.76 for excellent teacher ($n = 227$), with a very small range of .4. The mean for excellent course rating was 4.29, with response rates hovering around 75%. Common qualitative statements included statements such as "you are perfect!" "She was an awesome teacher that I enjoyed having as a professor" and finally,

is by far one of the best professors. She is extremely active and engaging with students and course material. It is obvious that she enjoys teaching and has a great passion for learning. She makes students WANT to do well.

In contrast, my online ratings provided a very different vision. Using the same Likert scale with 1 = low and 5 = high, my average was 3.78 for excellent teacher, while the excellent course rating average was 3.2 for the mere 19 students who filled out the evaluations across the three summer semesters. The response rate average for the online courses was 27%. The discrepancies in my evaluations between modalities were obvious. Although the decrease in ratings online matched with the propositions found in some other studies (Baker, 2010; Lyke & Frank, 2012; Rothman et al., 2011), it was important to identify the potential cause for the discrepancies and to explore solutions.

Shortly after receiving the poor course evaluations one summer, an unscheduled meeting with a student caused an epiphany. After spending the better part of an hour with "Ann," the name of the student finally clicked: she was one of the students who had just completed the online statistics class. When I met her in the live setting, I found her to be completely dynamic, full of energy and vitality, with lots of personality. That is when I realized that I never "got" Ann; her personality was not allowed to shine in its bright capacity in the asynchronous online environment. When I met her in the live setting, she was as articulate as in her online persona, but so much more. My epiphany was twofold, as I also hypothesized that neither Ann nor her classmates "got" me either. I too, am a vivacious person with a passion for student learning. The asynchronous environment again squashed the students' perception of how much I care, despite multiple e-mails stating such facts.

With this story and general context in mind, I hoped to circumvent the disconnection by holding synchronous sessions to teach, answer questions, build rapport, and otherwise bond with students in an upcoming online statistics class. The literature supported my hypothesis that increasing the number and quality of student/faculty interactions and responses into real time would provide for a greater sense of engagement, satisfaction, and perceived learning (Allen et al., 2002; Falloon, 2011; Hrastinski, 2008; Swan, 2002). Schutt, Allen, and Laumakis (2009) encouraged the addition of synchronous activities, and others offered its enhancement of student outcomes (Dickey, 2003; Shotsberger, 2000). Additionally, Parenti (2013) listed student preferences for live synchronous class time sessions, live synchronous chat messaging, as well as keeping the standard asynchronous e-mail communications. I adhered to all such advice with the thought that by adding synchronous learning to the course structure, I could get to know the students better and that they would truly see how much I care and my passion for their learning. I hoped that this would translate into greater degrees of learning and associated satisfaction with the course and my teaching, per general common sense as well as the literature.

Unfortunately, once mentored through using the synchronous materials and implementing them during the online summer session, I found my results to be similar to previous semesters. The actual results were 3.4 for excellent teacher and 3.3 for the progress on relevant objectives. In short, the excellent teacher rating went down, and the excellent course rating increased, though only slightly. Holding the live synchronous sessions might have helped, but not greatly. One student commented that "The coursework was challenging but the weekly live sessions definitely helped." For others, however, the live sessions did not change the students' perceptions of learning, nor their perceptions of me:

[She] is quite possibly the worst professor I have come across in my academic and professional career. She made the subject dry and difficult and outside of setting up a 1 hour tutor session every Thursday, she hardly helped in getting through the subject ... made this subject so difficult that I had to take time

from other courses just to balance her workload. She overly criticized every assignment I completed and made an entry level course into the most difficult subject I have ever come across. I would not recommend her to anyone.

I could write a whole dissertation defending myself from the student above, but suffice it to say that provisions were made to support the student in every capacity available: extended deadlines, mastery learning approaches, frequent encouraging messages through the class announcements page, a daily answer to questions posted in the specific help forum, and so forth. However, the notion that I must defend my actions just further exemplifies my position that the students did not feel the support that I was offering. Despite the live sessions, it was not enough to build the support, rapport, and trust necessary for optimal student success in the difficult content area.

While the results of my synchronous experiment neither demonstrated any evaluative improvement in the sample nor could they be inferred to the population due to the very limited sample sizes, they are still results worthy of reflection. The literature is fairly clear that the content area is generally rated lower than other coursework (Cashin, 1990, 1995; Constand & Pace, 2014; Felton, Koper, Mitchell, & Stinson, 2008; Royal & Stockdale, 2015), but as the content remained identical in level, instructor, assignments, and so forth, the validation of quantitative subject matter is moot. However, a reflective extension is to call for further research to compare all quantitative courses taught online at the university and/or the comparison of teaching evaluation scores of all professors who use the live, synchronous component available in the learning management system. A larger group of students might show that teaching synchronously is a benefit to students' perceptions of learning.

In conclusion, the changes to the class learning platform from asynchronous to synchronous, are inconclusive due to the low response rate and the small sample size. However, when I teach online again, I will continue the use of the synchronous component as I do feel that students gain greater benefits exemplified by a student comment on a course evaluation: "You can't ask the video a question." The synchronous format cannot be mandated due to our current marketing strategy for online education, but it is still the right thing to do, even if only on a voluntary student basis. For the time being, I will keep trying to enhance the connections between students, mathematical content, and myself in a synchronous environment, and spread the word of its potential benefits, that "when students are more active in the learning process, the material becomes more relevant and more significant for them, they remember it better, understand it and as a result their achievements improve" (Offir et al., 2008, p. 1181)

REFERENCES

Allen, M., Bourhis, J., Burrell, N., & Mabry, E. (2002). Comparing student satisfaction with distance education to traditional classroom in higher education: A meta-analysis. *The American Journal of Distance Education, 16*, 83–97.

Baker, C. (2010). The impact of instructor immediacy and presence for online student affective learning, cognition, and motivation. *The Journal of Educators Online, 7*(1), 1–30.

Berge, Z., & Meyers, B. (2000). Evaluating computer mediated communication courses in higher education. *Journal of Computing Research, 23*(4), 431–450.

Clark, R. E. (1994). Media will never influence learning. *Educational Technology Research and Development, 41*(2), 21–29.

Constand, R. L., & Pace, R. D. (2014). Student evaluations of finance faculty: Perceived difficulty means lower faculty evaluations. *Journal of Financial Education, 40*, 14–44.

Cole, J. E., & Kritzer, J. B. (2009). Strategies for success: Teaching an online course. *Rural Special Education Quarterly, 28*(4), 36–40.

Dickey, M. D. (2003). Teaching in 3D: Pedagogical affordances and constraints of 3D virtual worlds for synchronous distance learning. *Distance Education, 24*, 105–121.

Falloon, G. (2011). Making the connection: Moore's theory of transactional distance and its relevance to the use of a virtual classroom in postgraduate online teacher education. *Journal of Research in Technology in Education, 43*(3), 187–209.

Felton, J., Koper, P. T., Mitchell, J. B., & Stinson, M. (2008). Attractiveness, easiness, and other issues: Student evaluations of professors on RateMyProfessors.com. *Assessment and Evaluation in Higher Education, 33*, 45–61.

Hrastinski, S. (2008). Asynchronous and synchronous e-learning. A study of asynchronous and synchronous e-learning methods discovered that each supports different purposes. *Educause Quarterly, 31*(4), 51–55.

IDEA. (n.d.). Retrieved from http://www.ideaedu.org/

Lyke, J. & Frank, M. (2012). Comparison of student learning outcomes in online and traditional classroom environments in a psychology course. *Journal of Instructional Psychology, 39*(4), 245–264.

Kirk, F. R., & Spector, C. A. (2009). A comparison of the achievement of students taught by full-time versus adjunct faculty in business courses. *Academy of Education Leadership Journal, 13*(2), 73–80.

Mueller, B., Mandernach, B. J., & Sanderson, K. (2013). Adjunct versus full-time faculty: comparison of student outcomes in the online classroom. *MERLOT Journal of Online Teaching and Learning, 9*(3), 341–352.

Offir, B., Lev, Y. & Bezalel, R. (2008). Surface and deep learning processes in distance education: Synchronous versus asynchronous systems. *Computers & Education, 51*, 1172–1183.

Parenti, M. A. (2013). Student perceptions of asynchronous and synchronous web based tools and perceived attainment of academic outcomes. *Journal of Educational Technology, 9*(4), 8–14.

Rothman, T., Romeo, L., Brennan, M., & Mitchell, D. (2011). Criteria for assessing student satisfaction with online courses. *International Journal for e-Learning Security, 1*(1/2), 27–32.

Royal, K. D., & Stockdale, M. R. (2015). Are teacher course evaluations biased against faculty that teach quantitative methods courses? *International Journal of Higher Education, 4*(1), 217–224.

Schutt, M., Allen, B. S., & Laumakis, M. A. (2009). The effects of instructor immediacy behaviors in online learning environments. *Quarterly Review of Distance Education, 10*(2), 135–148.

Shotsberger, P. G. (2000). The human touch: Synchronous communication tools in web-based
learning. *Educational Technology, 40*(1), 53–56.
Swan, K. (2001). Virtual interaction: Design factors
affecting student satisfaction and perceived
learning in asynchronous online courses. *Distance Education, 22*(2), 306–331.

CHANGE AGENTS AND OPINION LEADERS
Integration of Classroom Technology

Christopher Masullo
Passaic County Community College

This study investigated 10 public elementary schools that employed district technology coordinators to facilitate the implementation of classroom technologies. These technology coordinators act as change agents who sought out classroom teachers to serve as opinion leaders. These opinion leaders had the ability to influence the attitudes and beliefs of their colleagues with regards to which technologies were used and how they were implemented to enhance learning. The purpose of this study was to investigate how technology coordinators identified and selected classroom teachers as opinion leaders as well as the perceptions of the opinion leader's colleagues. Using a qualitative study design, data were collected using structured data-collection instruments. An analysis of the data in this study supported the claim that technology coordinators were, for the most part, able to identify technology opinion leaders in their schools, but still overlook some potential leaders.

A nationwide emphasis on raising student achievement as well as teacher accountability has increased interest in studying school improvement and effective classroom instruction. Studies revealed that when it comes to school improvement, leadership matters (Gaziel, 2007; Hallinger & Heck, 1998, Marzano, Waters, & McNulty, 2005). Closing the gaps between what teachers are presenting and what students already know suggests the need to increase technology leadership knowledge and skills that go beyond the basics (Schrum, Galizio, & Ledesma, 2011). U.S. schools have invested billions of dollars on computer hardware and software (Compass Intelligence,

2010) due to the potential of technology to improve classroom instruction and student performance (Collins & Halverson, 2009; Zucker, 2008).

When it comes to how best to use these technologies to enhance learning and improve student performance, teachers look to an instructional leader to guide them in the implementation of these programs. Despite the abundance of knowledge on educational leadership, there is little known about the potential role of the technology coordinator as a change agent and the use of classroom teachers as opinion leaders to infuse technology into the teaching process. There has been little research

• **Christopher Masullo**, 121 William Street, Nutley, NJ 07110. Telephone: (973) 337-7407. E-mail: christophermasullo @verizon.net

The Quarterly Review of Distance Education, Volume 18(2), 2017, pp. 57–71
ISSN 1528-3518

on leadership in the area of technology (McLeod & Richardson, 2011) and even less research on how leaders demonstrate the extent technology can be used to support instructional innovation and improve teaching strategies (Dexter, 2011). A lack of research exists on the role that informal leaders, opinion leaders, and change agents play in the adoption of technological innovations in education (Ng'ambi & Bozalek, 2013). This study sought to address the gap in the research literature.

Technology leadership is necessary for the effective utilization of technology in schools (Anderson & Dexter, 2005). Anderson and Dexter (2005) concluded that although technology infrastructure is important, in order for educational technology to become an integral part of a school, technology leadership is even more so. This is because technology leadership has greater impact on outcomes.

Schools are implementing virtual classrooms, robotics, one-to-one mobile devices, and adopting digital versions of textbooks. There is also a surge in the assimilation of science, technology, engineering, and math (STEM) lesson planning. Teachers of technology have the responsibilities of meeting the Common Core Standards and preparing their students for state testing. With the addition of these technologies come great responsibilities and the need for leadership (Merisotis & Kee, 2006).

The effective technology leader should possess certain qualities and characteristics. School leaders should have a clear vision on how technology will be used to support teaching and learning. Technology plans should be developed and periodically revised to incorporate ever-evolving programs. As hardware and software advances, instructional leaders need to make access to technology readily available to staff and students. It is the leader's responsibility to model effective technology usage as well as monitor and evaluate the integration of technology as to its effectiveness. Leaders in technology need to provide training and support to staff and establish policies to address the ethical and legal issues involved in the use

of technology in schools. A leader of technology education should possess a clear vision of how the technology should be implemented as well as pay attention to the culture of leadership (Brown University, 2008).

Leadership is regarded as a process of giving direction to a group and the leader is identified on the basis of his or her relationship with others in the social group who are the followers. The leader, therefore, is in an emerging rather than predefined role, which can only be understood through examining the relationships within the group.

Administrators, particularly principals or directors of curriculum, have the title and responsibility of being the leader of instruction for schools. But, because these leaders are not in the classroom, they do not have as close a connection with the classroom teacher as does the technology teacher. Principals and directors are not always aware of the challenges faced by teachers. They do not always know of all the available technologies and how best to use them. Mundy and Kupczynski (2013) noted,

> Despite overall increased access to technology both in and out of the classroom, technology is often still not being used to support learning and instruction in a meaningful manner. Teachers need to be helped to change the way they teach rather than just how to use computers. (p. 1)

For these reasons, leadership is necessary for the effectiveness and sustainability of school technology programs.

Many times, the people given the title of administrator of the district or school are not prepared or qualified to be leaders in technology. The technology coordinators and classroom teachers are in a position to have direct knowledge of the available technology. They are most often the ones keeping up-to-date with the ever-evolving devices and software. The technology teachers are in close contact with students and fellow teachers. They know firsthand the challenges faced by their colleagues.

Districts have a vested interest in sustaining the programs for which they have budgeted. Now, more than ever, we need the opinion leaders of technology to step up as leaders to support and guide teachers.

Many theories are emerging that contradict traditional thinking about leadership roles. These theories suggest the technology teacher can and should be considered a leader and not doing so actually hinders progress.

This discussion progresses from the importance of leadership in technology to the characteristic of a good leader and the roles various leaders play in technology implementation as well as the roles played by positional leaders as well as opinion leaders. This study examined the relative roles of the technology coordinator, the classroom teachers who used technology, and the opinion leaders who influenced them.

THE PROBLEM

According to Murphy (2001), "The problem with educational leadership preparation programs today is that they are driven by neither education nor leadership" (p. 14) but rather by economic, social, and political forces. Most states and institutions do not require any formal preparation concerning technology education or training for educators unless that is their area of certification, nor do states require school leaders to demonstrate knowledge or skills that encourage technology preparation for classroom teachers. Graduates in the education field are most likely ill-prepared to implement technology in their school districts (Schrum et al., 2011).

It is for these reasons it is critical for the technology coordinators/facilitators working in school districts to act as agents of change. As change agents, they can recognize and engage classroom teachers who serve as opinion leaders for their colleagues. Due to their technical credibility and trustworthiness as representatives of the group, others gravitate towards opinion leaders (Leonard-Barton &

Kraus, 1985). These opinion leaders are informal leaders who have the ability to influence the attitudes and behaviors of others (Rogers & Kincaid, 1981).

The purpose of this study was to investigate opinion leadership and the role of the technology coordinator as the change agent within a public school system with regards to technology implementation. This study examined the role of the technology educator as a change agent with regards to the choice and implementation of technology in a public elementary school setting. The opinions of technology coordinators, facilitators, and classroom teachers were examined for similarities and differences as to who they perceived as the technology opinion leader. It explored the factors that contributed to the classroom teacher being an effective opinion leader with regards to technology usage and implementation. The focus of the study was to identify the technology coordinator as a change agent and how he or she identified a classroom teacher as an opinion leader for the implementation of technology in the teaching/learning process. This study explored the process by which the technology coordinator selected classroom teacher-opinion leaders to diffuse technology education and whether these selections agreed with who the survey instruments identified as opinion leaders according to Rogers' (2003) definition.

IMPORTANCE OF A TECHNOLOGY LEADER

According to Puckett (2014), "A leader must expect excellence; however, (s)he must also display excellence" (p. 1). There are many leadership types and some leaders possess qualities that fit scenarios better. Studies suggested school and district policies, practices, and leadership can have an impact on the scope and manner in which teachers use technology (O'Dwyer, Russell, & Bebell, 2004).

According to Anderson and Dexter (2005), leadership is the key to promoting teacher's use of technology. Dawson and Rakes (2003) found that many principals were uniformed and uninvolved in the role of technology in their schools. The principal is the assigned leader by position and title but because technology has such an impact on our lives, the technology coordinator is better equipped to impact change in the areas where technology directly impacts the teachers and students (Lai, Trewern, & Pratt, 2002).

Fullan (2002) acknowledged, "Effective school leaders are key to large-scale, sustainable education reform" (p. 16). Katzenmeyer and Moller (2001) concluded that reform takes place when teacher-leaders are allowed to flourish.

Technology support is important, but technology leadership is a stronger predictor of teacher use of computers in the classroom (Anderson & Dexter, 2005).

The opinion leader teachers who use technology are beneficial for assisting their fellow teacher. They guide others by demonstrating the different ways technology can be infused into the classroom learning environment. They are the teachers other staff members look to for support and ideas, but the technology resource teachers, themselves, do not always receive adequate support. Teachers, in order to integrate technology effectively, require support in the way of time, resources, and leadership (Strudler, Falba, & Hearington, 2003).

The influence of the technology coordinator is also critical. The school's technology infrastructure, teacher skill and confidence level, and provisions of professional development are responsibilities normally assigned to the coordinator; however, little research has explored this role (McGarr & McDonagh, 2014).

Technology is a unique subject in that it is included in all other disciplines in some form or another. To prepare students for future education and the world of work, technology has to be infused into all areas of the curriculum. Teachers in self-contained classrooms require guidance and modeling to assist them in integrating subjects (Ramirez, 2011).

These responsibilities then become the charge of the technology coordinator. When the technology coordinator is perceived as a change agent, he or she will be able to promote the types of technology and the way these technologies are used in the lessons. Many teachers rely on their colleagues for technology support because they are on site and have knowledge of the curriculum and classroom (Dexter, Anderson, & Ronnkvist, 2002). Rogers (2003) said these technology teachers may not be in administrative positions but still promote technology integration at the classroom level because they are similar to the people they are helping.

The classroom teacher needs to be included in the technology leadership process. Technology coordinators explore the best ways to identify the opinion leaders who will set the example of how to incorporate technology into their students' education. They are the workers in most direct contact with their colleagues and students. It is for these reasons further research into the nature of technology leadership is necessary (Langran, 2010; Sugar & Holloman, 2009).

ROLE OF THE TECHNOLOGY LEADER

Despite the efforts of schools, their technology integration is limited by their inability to individualize teachers' learning about how to integrate technology effectively into their teaching. Also, schools typically fail to provide feedback to teachers on their technology integration efforts in the form of peer coaching (Dexter, 2011). According to Ng'ambi and Bozalek (2013), "For emerging technologies to be diffused in institutional social systems, more transformational and less transactional leadership is required.... Leveraging informal leadership is particularly critical in accelerating the uptake of emerging technologies practices" (p. 940).

An example of distributed leadership in the realm of educational technology is the position of the technology coordinator (Lai & Pratt, 2004). The technology coordinator position is described as a "position with a protocol" (Frazier & Bailey, 2004, p. 1). The responsibilities of the technology coordinator extends to include instructing teachers about technology, solving technical problems for teachers, providing access to technological resources, and collaborating with teachers to develop curriculum and materials to be used in the classroom (Sugar, 2005).

Formal leaders tend to have an internal institutional focus as their main directive, while change agents and opinion leaders use technologies external to the institution to improve practices (Ng'ambi & Bozalek, 2013). Thus, formal leaders need to work with opinion leaders to ensure management of institutions has heightened awareness of changes and innovations (Williams, Karousou, & Mackness, 2011). In effect, there needs to be a top-down, bottom-up, or distributed approach for the diffusion of technological ideas to occur (Ng'ambi & Bozalek, 2013).

The use of informal leaders is needed to infuse innovative practices (D'Andrea & Gosling, 2005). Formal leaders should collaborate with opinion leaders and be responsive to a wide range of change agents in the institution. Opinion leaders are beneficial to the process of communication and influencing innovative practices in education (Ng'ambi & Bozalek, 2013).

THE TECHNOLOGY COORDINATOR AS A CHANGE AGENT

A change agent is a person who influences a client's decisions to adopt innovations. The technology supervisor, technology coordinator, and/or technology teacher, acting as a change agent, comes equipped with the degree and experience in the technology field. These change agents have solutions and ideas for improving classroom management and instruction using technology that may appeal to the teachers. In order to promote the infu-

sion of these ideas and overcome obstacles of teacher fears and uncertainties, the technology change agent may further distribute leadership responsibilities by employing the use of opinion leaders. Rogers (2003) noted,

> Diffusion campaigns are more likely to be successful if change agents identify and mobilize opinion leaders ... [and] change agents' success in securing the adoption of innovations by clients is positively related to the extent that he or she works through opinion leaders. (p. 388)

The traditional classroom of yesteryear saw the teacher presenting the contents of the syllabus, relying heavily on the textbook, and giving little consideration to the needs of the learner (Okojie, 2011). Today, teachers' roles have become more complex. Teachers are required to know their subject matter but also possess technological skills and play the roles of instructional method specialists and technology education researchers (Okojie, 2011). With the infusion of technology as a classroom learning tool, teachers' responsibilities have expanded. They are expected to seek solutions through critical thinking and challenging students to use a problem-solving approach. In this sense, teachers of technology assume the role of change agents (Okojie, 2011).

Computer teachers are needed who are willing to integrate technology in the classroom, keep up with innovations, and provide students the opportunities to use new technologies (Cakir & Yildirim, 2009; Göktas & Topu, 2012; Seferoğlu, 2007). Niess (2008) emphasized, "Tomorrow's teachers must be prepared to rethink, unlearn and relearn, change, revise, and adapt" (p. 225). In preparing teachers for technology integration, leaders must establish a vision, set expectations, and track progress toward that vision. Leaders must develop members' capacity by modeling and providing support (Thomas, Herring, Redmond, & Smaldino, 2013).

In most schools, the technology coordinator holds leadership responsibility but may not actually be an administrator. Their actual titles vary from district to district—from coordinator to director to specialist (Frazier & Bailey, 2004). The coordinator's role has shifted from technically supporting teachers in a lab to promoting technology-enhanced lessons in the classroom (Glazer & Page, 2006). Lobos (2008) noted,

> The first conclusion, as obvious as it may seem, is that coordinators are, at the same time, teachers who work in the same school and have been part of the faculty for several years. This is a very important issue that is not mentioned very often. Sometimes it seems natural and we take it for granted. However, this situation allows the introduction of new elements into school environments. Coordinators have taken part in the creation and redesign of cultural statutes, they are familiar with those statutes, and that makes them change agents. (p. 12)

A technology coordinator serves as an instructional expert by providing advice on how to incorporate technology effectively into a lesson (Sugar & Holloman, 2009). Twomey, Shamburg, and Zieger (2006) defined *technology coordinators* as those who "apply and implement curriculum plans that include methods and strategies for utilizing technology to maximize student learning" (p. 25). Technology coordinators need to be technical experts and capable of maintaining equipment as well as evaluating, purchasing, and informing teachers about new products (Twomey et al., 2006). Technology coordinators are expected to develop, assess, and lead technology initiatives (Sugar & Holloman, 2009). The technology coordinator plays a major role in the planning and implementation of technology, serves as a change agent, and provides professional development for his or her colleagues (Lai et al., 2002).

THE ROLE OF TECHNOLOGY OPINION LEADERSHIP

Opinion leadership is the degree to which an individual is able to influence the attitudes and behaviors of others. Opinion leadership is not attached to the individual's status or formal position. Opinion leadership is qualified by the individual's technical proficiency and social accessibility and they serve as a model for their followers (Rogers, 2003). Rogers (2003) acknowledged, "The success or failure of diffusion programs rest in part on the role of opinion leaders" (p. 99).

Opinion leaders are informal leaders. They are members of the social system and earn the respect of others and serve as models. In the case of this study, opinion leaders are probably elementary teachers located in the school district in close contact with the technology-coordinator change agent. According to Rogers (2003), a diffusion campaign is more likely to be successful if the change agent is able to identify and properly use the opinion leader. Rogers said, "Change agents' success in securing the adoption of innovations by clients is positively related to the extent that he or she works through opinion leaders" (p. 388). By harnessing the potential influence of these teacher opinion leaders, the technology change agent can increase the rate at which innovations can be diffused throughout the elementary school. Rogers set forth several adopter categories. The "early adopters" are more integrated into the local social system than innovators and have the highest degree of leadership (Rogers, 2003).

Larson and Meyer (2006) explained,

> Faculty become aware of and are influences to adopt, or not, an innovation through communication.... At the persuasion stage— when potential adopters are forming or changing attitudes—it is interpersonal channels that involve a face-to-face exchange that are of greater importance. (p. 79)

In their study of the diffusion of STEM pedagogies, Larson and Meyer suggested that "for opinion leaders to influence others to use new pedagogical practices, they themselves must 'buy' into the innovation and feel compelled to tell others" (p. 85). To influence others to adopt innovative practices, opinion leaders can exercise more active influential strategies such as seminars, mentoring, or personalized discussions, as well as less active strategies such as letter or e-mail correspondence directing clients to a website.

Change agents can track the following steps to promote an innovation: create awareness of the innovation, strategically identify one faculty member believed to be particularly influential, provide incentives like extra time or reduced workload to allow for the implementation of new practices, encourage faculty to share their experiences at meetings and workshops, and assess results of and record data to show the resulting outcomes and benefits of learning (Larson & Meyer, 2006). The effective use of opinion leaders will accelerate and increase adoption as well as use interpersonal communication to reduce potential adopter's uncertainty associated with innovations.

Technology resource teachers have been able to act as change agents in schools. The technology resource teacher can inspire other teachers with a vision of how to implement technology effectively by demonstrating activities the classroom teacher can use. Technology resource teachers also can relate to classroom teachers as a fellow professional who understands their situation. (Frazier & Bailey, 2004). Technology resource teachers can be leaders based on their position or the knowledge they possess (Leithwood & Riehl, 2003). If technology teachers are not given the opportunity to assume a leadership role, the ability of the school to sustain innovation becomes hindered (Langran, 2010).

According to Larson and Meyer (2006), faculty may learn about new pedagogies from websites, journals, and workshops but are more likely to be persuaded to try these pedagogies through interpersonal communication with an opinion leader. The ability to reduce the perceived risk and uncertainty associated with adopting new innovations is through the interpersonal communication and influence of the opinion leader (Rogers, 2003).

Riveros, Newton, and da Costa (2013) identified emerging themes shared by teacher-leaders. They generally arise from informal processes in their schools. Teacher-leaders develop a broader understanding of educational leadership as they begin to work outside their own classroom and are recruited into broader leadership roles. Teacher-leaders require structures that allow them to facilitate trust and collegiality with their peers.

As mentors and leaders, teachers of technology can help other teachers overcome barriers to technology integration (Kopcha, 2010). Twomey et al. (2006) offered the following:

> Technology facilitators and technology leaders shoulder the responsibility to keep abreast of current trends and future prospects, mediating between all of the stakeholders. They are the proponents of technology who constantly look for new ideas and information to share with the teachers in their schools. In return, they must be able to teach technology skills as well as understand ways to utilize technology to support instructional goals. (p. 116)

Twomey et al. further offered,

> District technology leaders have the most influential voice in district technology decisions. To create and sustain a vision for integrating technology into teaching and learning, districts need to create full-time positions for technology leaders. This position should be deeply involved in the district's educational goals and strategies. Investing in technology leadership will foster a strong culture to support more effective integration of technology into the schools. (p. 124)

In some instances, faculty members have reported that they would not have taken risks or attempted new technology projects had it not been for the technology leader. The faculty preferred to receive assistance from the teacher-leader (Lundeberg Tikoo, & Willers, & Donley, 2004).

METHODOLOGY

The technology coordinators were surveyed as to whom they saw as the classroom teacher-opinion leaders in the schools they served. All teachers in the service of the technology coordinator were also administered a survey to determine how well they fit the profile of opinion leader and if these were, in fact, the same people the change agent identified as an opinion leader.

Participants

One technology coordinator was surveyed in each of 10 school districts. A typical elementary school consisted of Kindergarten through Grade 6, with two sections at each grade. Approximately 10 teachers were surveyed per school. After 10 schools were evaluated, the total number of participants was 105. All participants were employees of the public school systems. Participants were male and female elementary certified teachers and administrators ranging in age from 25–65 years old with at least 5 years of teaching experience.

The first group consisted of the technology coordinators (change agents). One technology coordinator and or technology supervisor was selected from each of the 10 school districts. A questionnaire was issued to the technology coordinator containing questions regarding his or her background, education, and who he or she regarded as the opinion leader in their school.

The second group consisted of the classroom teachers who used technology in their lessons and activities. These teachers worked in the school and were in direct contact with the technology coordinator. The technology coordinator provided a list of these staff members. The classroom teachers were surveyed using an innovativeness scale and a local expert profile at their respective schools. This group was a volunteer sampling as not all teachers may have agreed to participate in the surveys. These teachers were surveyed to determine the opinion leaders of the group.

Data-Collection Instruments

The district technology coordinator was issued the Technology Coordinator Survey. The Technology Coordinator Survey was adapted from the Boston Society for Information Management as well as the studies by Cox-Cruey (1998). It used a Likert-type scale with demographic questions dealing with the technology coordinator's responsibilities and role as a change agent and the factors contributing to their success.

The second survey, an Opinion Leadership Scale (Wright, Ryan, Dodge, Last, & Law, 2004), was used to question the technology coordinator as to whom he or she identified as the opinion leader. The Opinion Leadership Scale was modified from the Hiss, MacDonald, and Davis (1978) original.

A Local Expert Profile (LEP, Rice, 1994) was used to identify elementary classroom teachers as opinion leaders. A LEP is a self-reporting instrument designed to identify those individuals who serve as local experts. In the case of this study, the local experts were the classroom teachers who used the technologies in their daily teaching activities. This study used a LEP as a self-reporting instrument to verify the classroom teacher-opinion leaders. The LEP instrument consisted of 25 multiple-choice questions presented as categorical with Likert scale ranges.

The Innovativeness Scale, developed by Hurt, Joseph, and Cook (1977), was the second instrument employed to identify the opinion leaders. The Innovativeness Scale (Hurt et al., 1977) is a self-reporting instrument consisting of 20 items in a Likert-type scale and used to measure an individual's innovativeness based on Rogers' (2003) categories of adopters: innovators, early adopters, early majority, late majority, and laggards.

The Innovativeness Scale was issued to the teachers on staff in the elementary schools. This self-reporting survey assessed the extent to which the teacher fit the description of an opinion leader. The opinion leaders were those surveyed in the "early majority" section of the scale.

RESULTS

The study asked, "What do you think is the most important responsibility for the technology coordinator/facilitator as a change agent?" Responses were as follows:

The most important responsibility as a change agent is to stay current with technology and best practices. It is then their responsibility to share those techniques and ideas with the staff. They can do this through videotaping, blogging about it, modeling, or giving workshops.

Teachers are required to attend technology classes with their students, and since we will have a one-to-one initiative in Grades 4–6 next year, I think it is important for teachers to reinforce skills learned in class. I also try to introduce projects that can be integrated into any subject area, especially math and science. My curriculum is actually directly tied in with the science standards.

It is my job to help the staff, teachers, and students embrace change as technology moves around us very quickly. I must be one step ahead of the others with the new software and hardware available on a daily basis. It is equally important for me to figure out how these changes impact our daily school routines and balance this so it does not seem like an issue while implementing the change.

Visionary Leadership. Stated by Shanker & Sayeed (2012) where "Leadership can be defined as a social process of influencing other people's orientation towards achievement of goals, it is a style that evolves itself around organizational change process directly and transforms individuals" (p. 470). Accordingly, visionary leadership is the single most crucial activity for a technology change agent. See also: http://www.cosn.org/VisionToAction

"To be at the forefront of emerging technology and explaining why the district needs to the new technology."

"To help the community be aware of what we are doing with the students in school, and to keep everyone on the same page."

"The role of technology coordinator is very different in every district. Change is difficult. I rely on my 'heavy hitters' to buy in to something and I support them... then others follow."

"To work with the stakeholders in the district to understand that education is fluid system that is constantly changing and that we as a district need to be able to adapt and change with it."

"Helping other teachers implement technology to enhance learning and not for the sake of using technology."

The study also asked, **"Who are the technology opinion leaders in your public school system and what characteristics do they have in common?"** The technology coordinators/facilitators were asked to name the teachers they saw as the technology opinion leaders in their schools. The LEP was then used to identify elementary classroom teachers as opinion leaders. This self-reporting instrument was designed to identify those individuals who served as local experts. In the case of this study, the local experts were the classroom teachers using the technologies in their regular teaching. The LEP consisted of a series of survey questions issued to the teachers who were in contact with the technology coordinator.

The highest possible score on the LEP (after weighting was considered) was 750 and the lowest score was 175. The local experts shared the same characteristics (perception of the innovation, venturesomeness, cosmopoliteness, connection to the social system, and experience with an innovation) as the early adopters/opinion leaders.

A third question asked, "How do these opinion leaders assist you in classroom technology infusion?"

Technology coordinators and facilitators responded as follows:

1. "They offer to share their lessons and ideas that they try in the classroom. They spread the word and are positive when they speak to others."
2. Another technology coordinator/facilitator responded, "They give their insights and opinions on hardware and software that will be best used in the classroom. They also try out new technology and provide important feel back after they tested new technologies with their students and they seek out new forms of technology to be used. These teachers are not afraid of trying new things."
3. "They all look for ways to incorporate technologies that enhance learning."
4. "Yes, they help keep the equipment working well with our curriculum needs."
5. "They are willing to learn and to train others."
6. "The opinion leaders are the teachers that pilot program and initiative as well as being lead teachers at schools to provide assistance with technology questions or issues."
7. "Having just been in the district a year, and reporting to the BA as the 'tech operations guy,' I am not sure I am yet aware of the technology opinion leaders in my district. Still working on this."
8. "When others see the opinion leader using the technology and how the technology makes teaching more productive, they are more apt to implement it themselves."

A fourth question asked, "How do these technology opinion leaders influence other teachers in their use of classroom technology?"

Technology coordinators/facilitators were asked how the opinion leaders in their schools influenced other teachers and how they used classroom technology. The following are some of the responses:

1. "These teachers are willing to talk about what they do with technology. They show others and volunteer to do lessons in their classes. One teacher has done various workshops throughout the school year."
2. "As a power user."
3. "They share their expertize [sic] with various members of the staff and faculty and offer assistance when planning future purchases. Their willingness to try new ideas makes it easier for others to consider the same."
4. "They show how the technology can work and push others to use it."
5. "They teach, they problem solve, they provide the best equipment available."
6. "They assist teachers as needed. Teachers value their expertise."
7. "They are teacher-leaders at different schools who model the infusion for instructional technology in the classroom. Their dynamic teaching style engages the students."
8. "They are usually the first to buy-into the ideas of incorporation new technological resources and they set the examples for others to follow."

A fifth question asked, "Is there agreement in the view of the teachers and the technology coordinator with regard to choice of opinion leaders?" When the 10 districts from which classroom teachers responded are analyzed, a margin of error in each district can be seen. District A's technology coordinator/facilitator selected no opinion leaders and had no teachers ranking in the early adopter category, so there was an error of 0% in District A. The technology coordinator/facilitator in District B selected two of the four potential opinion leaders who did not rank in the early adopter scale giving that district an error rate of 50%. School District C missed 9 of its 13 leaders for an error of 69%. District D's technology coordinator/facilitator selected no opinion leaders and had no teachers ranking in the early adopter category, so there was an error of 0%. The technology coordinator in District E missed one of the two responding leaders for an error rate of 50%. District F's technology facilitator missed one out of the 13 responding teachers for an error rate of 8%. District G missed identifying two of its leaders for an error of 16%. District H's technology coordinator overlooked one leader and identified another incorrectly for an error rate of 25%. The technology coordinators in Districts I and J each overlooked one and incorrectly identified two opinion leaders for error ratings of 50% and 30%, respectively.

DISCUSSION

The LEP was implemented to collect data from the classroom teachers served by the technology coordinators/facilitators to determine if the teachers were, in fact, opinion leaders. Figure 1 displays a graphical representation of the data collected in this study compared to the normative data indicating a slight skew to the left. Rice (1994) indicated no one characteristic taken alone can be used to identify an opinion leader. It is for this reason all characteristics were totaled when scoring.

The Innovativeness Scale was incorporated to measure the innovativeness of the teachers. Figure 2 graphically depicts that the classroom teachers surveyed had a significantly lower percentage in the late majority category at 15% compared to the normative data at 34%. The study data revealed a higher percentage in the early majority category at 47% compared to the normative 24% and a higher percentage in the early adopter category at 26% compared to 14%.

When asked how the opinion leaders assisted with classroom technology infusion, technology coordinators/facilitators responded that classroom teacher-opinion leaders were those willing to share their lessons. These technology opinion leaders were also the ones who lent their insights on how best to use the hardware and software in the classroom. These teachers piloted programs and trained others.

When asked how the technology opinion leaders influenced others in the use of classroom technology, technology coordinators/facilitators responded that classroom teacher-opinion leaders were those who volunteered to

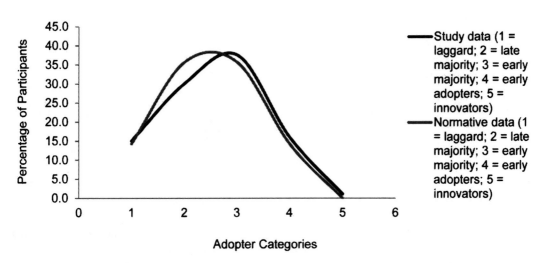

Source: Normative data obtained from Rice (1994).

FIGURE 1
Local Expert Profile Comparison of Study Data and Normative Data

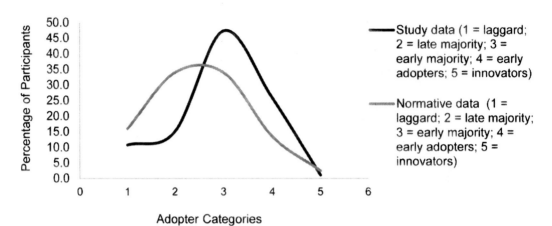

Source: Normative data obtained from Simonson (2000).

FIGURE 2

Innovativeness Scale Comparison of Study Data and Normative Data

do lessons in other classrooms. Their willingness to try new things made it easier for others to follow suit. Other teachers valued the expertise of these opinion leader teachers who set the example for others to follow.

When the selections made by the technology coordinators/facilitators were examined as to who they identified as opinion leaders, they selected a classroom teacher who scored as an opinion leader on the local expert profile, the innovativeness scale, or both a number of times. They were also incorrect a number of times when they chose a teacher who did not score as an opinion leader or overlooked one who did. All school respondents considered, the technology coordinators were correct on average about 70% of the time in the selection of a classroom teacher technology-opinion leader.

When all teacher respondents are considered by district, the classroom teachers surveyed selected the technology coordinator/facilitator as a technology opinion leader on average about 60% of the time. Also, the classroom teachers chose the same teacher opinion leaders as the technology coordinator/facilitator on average about 47% of the time.

CONCLUSIONS

This study found several important conclusions about change agents and opinion leaders. One result derived from this study was that although technology coordinators/facilitators are able to identify the teachers who qualify as opinion leaders an average of 70% of the time, they still overlooked some potential leaders at their respective schools. Technology coordinators/facilitators can periodically use surveys like those used in this research to identify opinion leaders formally as those leaders might change. Also, about 47% of the classroom teachers identified the same opinion leaders as the technology coordinators/facilitators. School district technology coordinators and leaders should research ways to best promote the classroom opinion leaders in an effort to make them more recognizable as valuable sources for other teaching staff. Technology coordinators/facilitators may choose to promote classroom opinion leaders by distributing leadership responsibilities to these teachers. Teacher opinion leaders could be asked to share ideas at faculty meetings and be given the opportunity to conduct workshops for other staff members.

The goal of this research was to add to the body of knowledge relating to the technology coordinator/facilitator's identification and use of technology opinion leaders in the best ways to integrate classroom technology. Classroom technology is ever-evolving and expanding. There will always be a need for the technology coordinator/facilitator change agent to be able to identify classroom-teacher opinion leaders.

REFERENCES

Anderson, R. E., & Dexter, S. (2005). School technology leadership: An empirical investigation of prevalence and effect. *Educational Administration Quarterly, 41*, 49–82. doi:10.1177/0013161X04269517

Brown University. (2008). *Overview of spotlight: Leadership principles in technology.* Retrieved from http://www.brown.edu/academics/education-alliance/sites/brown.edu.academics.education-alliance/files/uploads/KLOOM_tech_entire.pdf

Cakir, R., & Yildirim, S. (2009). What do computer teachers think about the factors affecting technology integration in schools? *İlköğretim Online, 8*, 952–964.

Collins, A. C., & Halverson, R. (2009). *Rethinking education in the age of technology: The digital revolution and schooling in America.* New York, NY: Teachers College Press.

Compass Intelligence. (2010). *U.S. education information technology expenditures by education level, 2009–2014.* Scottsdale, AZ: Author.

Cox-Cruey, T. (1998). District technology coordinators: Change agents in Kentucky's age of technology. *Dissertation Abstracts International, 59*(04), 1053. (UMI No. 9831360)

D'Andrea, V. M., & Gosling, D. (2005). *Improving teaching and learning: a whole institution approach.* Maidenhead, England: Open University Press.

Dawson, C., & Rakes, G. C. (2003). The influence of principals' technology training on the integration of technology into schools. *Journal of Research on Technology in Education, 36*, 29–49. doi:10.1080/15391523.2003.10782401

Dexter, S. (2011). School technology leadership: Artifacts in systems of practice. *Journal of School Leadership, 21*, 166–189.

Dexter, S. L., Anderson, R. E., & Ronnkvist, A. (2002). Quality technology support: What is it? Who has it? and What difference does it make? *Journal of Educational Computing Research, 26*, 265–285. doi:10.2190/WFRB-PE10-WAMJ-G2P1

Frazier, M., & Bailey, G. D. (2004). *The technology coordinator's handbook.* Eugene, OR: International Society for Technology in Education.

Fullan, M. (2002). The change leader. *Educational Leadership, 59*(8), 16–20.

Gaziel, H. H. (2007). Re-examining the relationship between principals' instructional/educational leadership and student achievement. *Journal of Social Sciences, 15*(1), 17–24.

Glazer, E. M., & Page, K. (2006). Collaborative apprenticeship. *Learning and Leading With Technology, 33*(8), 10–13.

Göktaş, Y., & Topu, B. (2012). ICT teachers' assigned roles and expectations from them. *Educational Sciences: Theory and Practice, 12*, 473–478.

Hallinger, P., & Heck, R. (1998). Exploring the principal's contribution to school effectiveness: 1980–1995. *School Effectiveness and School Improvement, 9*, 157–191. doi:10.1080/0924345980090203

Hiss, R. G., MacDonald, R., & Davis, W. K. (1978, October). *Identification of physician educational influentials in small community hospitals.* Paper presented at the 17th annual conference on Research in Medical Education, New Orleans, LA.

Hurt, H. T., Joseph, K., & Cook, C. D. (1977). Scales for the measurement of innovativeness. *Human Communication Research, 4*(2), 58–65.

Katzenmeyer, M., & Moller, G. (2001). *Awaking the sleeping giant: Helping teachers develop as leaders.* Thousand Oaks, CA: Corwin.

Kopcha, T. J. (2010). A systems-based approach to technology integration using mentoring and communities of practice. *Educational Technology Research and Development, 58*, 175–190. doi:10.1007/s11423-008-9095-4

Lai, K. W., & Pratt, K. (2004). Information communication technology (ICT) in secondary schools: The role of the computer coordinator. *British Journal of Educational Technology, 35*, 461–475. doi:10.1111/j.0007-1013.2004.00404.x

Lai, K., Trewern, A., & Pratt, K. (2002). Computer coordinators as change agents: Some New Zealand observations. *Journal of Technology and Teacher Education, 10*, 539–551.

Langran, E. (2010). Technology resource teachers as school leaders. *Journal of Technology Integration in The Classroom, 2,* 163–179.

Larson, S. R., & Meyer, G. (2006). Diffusing STEM pedagogies: The role of opinion leaders. *Metropolitan Universities, 17*(4), 77–91. Retrieved from ERIC database. (EJ878209)

Leithwood, K. A., & Riehl, C. (2003). *What we know about successful school leadership.* Philadelphia, PA: Temple University, Laboratory for Student Success.

Leonard-Barton, D., & Kraus, W. A. (1985, November/December). Implementing new technology. *Harvard Business Review, 102.* Retrieved from https://hbr.org/1985/11/implementing-new-technology/ar/8

Lobos, M. Q. (2008, July). *The coordinator's dilemma: Between an electronic janitor and a pedagogical leader.* Paper presented at Encuentro Internacional Educa, Zaragoza, Spain. Retrieved from ERIC database. (ED505661)

Lundeberg, M., Tikoo, S.-Y., Willers, R., & Donley, E. (2004). Technology leadership cadre: A mutually beneficial relationship. *Journal of Computing in Teacher Education, 21*(1), 33–39. doi:10.1080/10402454.2004.10784507

Marzano, R. J., Waters, T., & McNulty, B. A. (2005). *School leadership that works: From research to results.* Alexandria, VA: Association for Supervision and Curriculum Development.

McGarr, O., & McDonagh, A. (2014, March). The ICT coordinator: Technology champion or maintenance technician? *Implications for ICT leadership in schools. Proceedings of International Technology, Education and Development Conference* (pp. 1067–1074). Valencia, Spain. Available from http://library.iated.org/view/MCGARR2014ICT

McLeod, S., & Richardson, J. W. (2011). The dearth of technology leadership coverage. *Journal of School Leadership, 21,* 216–240.

Merisotis, J. P., & Kee, A. M. (2006). A model of success: The Model Institutions for Excellence program's decade of leadership in STEM education. *Journal of Hispanic Higher Education, 5*(3), 288–308.

Mundy, M., & Kupczynski, L. (2013). A qualitative study of technology integration into culture and sustainability in schools. *ISRN Education, 2013,* 1–6. doi:10.1155/2013/967610

Murphy, J. (2001, November). The changing face of leadership preparation. *School Administrator, 58*(10), 14–17.

Ng'ambi, D., & Bozalek, V. (2013). Leveraging informal leadership in higher education institutions: A case of diffusion of emerging technologies in a southern context. *British Journal of Educational Technology, 44,* 940–950. doi:10.1111/bjet.12108

Niess, M. L. (2008). Guiding preservice teacher in developing TPCK. In AACTE Committee on Innovation and Technology (Ed.), *Handbook of technological pedagogical content knowledge (TPCK) for educators* (pp. 223–250). New York, NY: Routledge.

O'Dwyer, L. M., Russell, M., & Bebell, D. J. (2004). Identifying teacher, school and district characteristics associated with elementary teachers' use of technology: a multilevel perspective. *Education Policy Analysis Archives, 12*(48), 1–16. Retrieved from http://epaa.asu.edu/epaa/v12n48/

Okojie, M. C. (2011). The changing roles of teachers in a technology learning setting. *International Journal of Instructional Media, 38*(1), 17–25.

Puckett, R. (2014). Leadership in educational technology. *Journal of Educational Technology, 10*(4), 1–5.

Ramirez, A., Jr. (2011). Technology planning, purchasing and training: How school leaders can help support the successful implementation and integration of technology in the learning environment. *Journal of Technology Integration in the Classroom, 3*(1), 67–73.

Rice, J. A. (1994). *The study of the selection of local experts for the diffusion of complex technology cluster innovations within an organization* (Doctoral dissertation, University of Florida). Retrieved from https://archive.org/stream/studyofselection00rice/studyofselection00rice_djvu.txt

Riveros, A., Newton, P., & da Costa, J. (2013). From teachers to teacher-leaders: A case study. *International Journal of Teacher Leadership, 4*(1), 1–15.

Rogers, E. M. (2003). *Diffusion of innovations* (5th ed.). New York, NY: Free Press.

Rogers, E. M., & Kincaid, D. L. (1981). *Communication networks: Toward a new paradigm for research.* New York, NY: Free Press.

Schrum, L., Galizio, L. M., & Ledesma, P. (2011). Educational leadership and technology integration: An investigation into preparation, experiences, and roles. *Journal of School Leadership, 21,* 241–261.

Seferoğlu, S. S. (2007). Primary school computer curriculum: A critical evaluation and problems faced during implementation. *Eurasian Journal of Educational Research, 29,* 99–111.

Shanker, M., & Sayeed, O. B. (2012). Role of transformational leaders as change agents: Leveraging effects on organizational climate. *The Indian Journal of Industrial Relations, 47*(3), 470–484.

Strudler, N., Falba, C., & Hearrington, D. (2001). *The evolving role of school-based technology coordinators in elementary programs.* Retrieved from http://www.amoyemaat.org/strudler.pdf

Sugar, W. (2005). Instructional technologist as a coach: Impact of a situated professional development program on teachers' technology use. *Journal of Technology and Teacher Education, 13,* 547–571.

Sugar, W., & Holloman, H. (2009). Technology leaders wanted: Acknowledging the leadership role of a technology coordinator. *Techtrends: Linking Research and Practice to Improve Learning, 53*(6), 66–75. doi:10.1007/s11528-009-0346-y

Thomas, T., Herring, M., Redmond, P., & Smaldino, S. (2013). Leading change and innovation in teacher preparation: A blueprint for developing TPACK ready teacher candidates. *Techtrends, 57*(5), 55–63. doi:10.1007/s11528-013-0692-7

Twomey, C., Shamburg, C., & Zieger, L. (2006). *Teachers as technology leaders: A guide to ISTE technology facilitation and technology leadership accreditation.* Eugene, OR: International Society for Technology in Education.

Williams, R., Karousou, R., & Mackness, J. (2011). Emergent learning and learning ecologies. *International Review of Research in Open and Distance Learning, 12*(3), 39–59. Retrieved from http://www.irrodl.org/index.php/irrodl/article/view/883/1824

Wright, F. C., Ryan, D. P., Dodge, J. E., Last, L. D., & Law, C. H. L. (2004). Identifying educationally influential specialist: Issues arising from the use of "classic" criteria. *Journal of Continuing Education in the Health Professions, 24,* 213–226. doi:10.1002/chp.1340240405

Zucker, A. (2008). *Transforming schools with technology.* Cambridge, MA: Harvard Education Press.

AN INTRODUCTION
TO DISTANCE EDUCATION IN JAPAN

Ray J. Amirault and Yusra Laila Visser, International Editors
Illinois State University

In the previous issue of the *Quarterly Review of Distance Education*, we began our new series on the state of distance learning around the globe with an examination of distance education in Saudi Arabia, including examination of a specific case of distance learning within the Saudi Arabia higher education context. As editors, we felt that the specific issues surrounding distance education in Saudi Arabia, which may be different than in other counties, made an examination of the Saudi Arabian context an excellent one on which to commence this series.

In this current issue, we move from the Middle East to the *Far* East to examine the use of distance education in what is one of the world's most technologically sophisticated counties: Japan. Until only very recently the second largest economy in the world, with a GDP of some 5 billion U.S. dollars per year (The World Bank, 2017), the word "Japan" conjures up in the mind of people everywhere names such as *Sony, Toshiba, Panasonic, Mitsubishi, Honda, Toyota, Yamaha,* and many others. But how does Japan's undeniable technological prowess translate into the use of technology for distance education? More broadly, what part of Japan's overall education sector employs distance education, and via what tools and approaches?

Our guest author examining distance education in Japan, Mayuko Nakamura, speaks to these issues. In preparation for this article, Nakamura interviewed key leaders in Japan's online education programs during her most recent visit to the country in the summer of 2017. Nakamura's contribution to this issue of *QRDE* is fascinating of its own accord, but also raises some interesting questions about the potential relationship between a country's technological infrastructure/capabilities and the amount of online education actually employed within that country. We encourage readers to reflect on this question while reading Nakamura's article. Thinking back to Ayshah Alahmari's article on Saudi Arabian distance education, and combining it with the Japanese case, we also encourage readers to not only consider how distance education is used in each country, but in comparison with *other* countries in order to develop a broader understanding of the differential motivations for a country's choices impacting the use of distance education. Indeed, as we proceed further into this series, it is our goal to build a well-rounded understanding of such questions

The Quarterly Review of Distance Education, Volume 18(3), 2017, pp. 73–74
Copyright © 2017 Information Age Publishing, Inc.

ISSN 1528-3518

as we continue to examine distance education in widely different country contexts.

REFERENCES

The World Bank. (2017). Country data: Japan. Retrieved from https://data.worldbank.org/country/japan

THE STATE OF DISTANCE EDUCATION IN JAPAN

Mayuko Nakamura
Illinois State University

Japan is famous for technological advancement, spanning from high-speed trains, the automobile industry, and medical equipment to portable gaming and music devices. With this wealth of sophisticated technology at its disposal, people outside of Japan often may assume that this technological prowess is also well integrated into every phase of Japanese people's lives, including the education system. In point of fact, however, the integration of technologies in Japanese education, particularly within the higher education segment, is far behind that of other highly developed countries. Japanese online education has therefore also been lagging due to the low adoption of technologies in Japanese higher education settings and various cultural challenges surrounding education and employment present in the country. This article presents a basic overview of the Japanese educational system, highlights two Japanese institutions that have "found their niche" within online and distance education and promising future outlooks for high-quality online education, and concludes with a brief examination of the pedagogical and cultural shifts and collaboration between government, industry, and higher education, which are all essential to make online education a viable option for Japan's future.

INTRODUCTION

Japan is a sovereign country in eastern Asia that has a long history of independent governance. Except for the post-World War II occupation by the U.S. military, Japan has enjoyed independence and has thereby developed its own unique culture, arts, and traditions. After World War II, Japan become renowned for advanced technology and manufacturing. Japan has a population of approximately 127 million, with a rapidly aging population; as of 2016, 27% of the Japanese population was 65 years or older (Central Intelligence Agency, 2017). An aging population has many implications for the Japanese economy and infrastructure, including a shrinking workforce and the burden of higher healthcare costs in coming years.

• **Mayuko Nakamura**, Faculty Development Coordinator and Adjunct Instructor of Psychology, Illinois State University. E-mail: mnakamu@Ilstu.edu

The Quarterly Review of Distance Education, Volume 18(3), 2017, pp. 75–87   ISSN 1528-3518

Although an economic downturn since the 1990s has had a negative impact on Japan's GDP, the country stood as the second-largest economy in the world, moving to third place only very recently, following the United States and China (World Bank, 2017). Dedicated workforce based on lifetime employment and strong government-industry cooperation likely have contributed to the success of its unique economy (Crawford, 1998). In April 2017, Japan's unemployment rate fell to 2.8%, the lowest in 2 decades, mainly due to the shrinking working-age population. Despite the low unemployment rate, however, many Japanese workers now suffer from underemployment. Green and Henseke (2016) analyzed 2013 Organization for Economic Co-operation and Development (OECD) data and reported that nearly 50% of college graduates are underemployed in Japan. Educating and reeducating Japan's future workforce is therefore a critically important task for the nation.

THE EDUCATIONAL SYSTEM OF JAPAN

Before moving into a discussion of online education in Japan, it is helpful to establish a basic understanding of the educational system in place in the country. A brief discussion of the Japanese P–16 education system provides the context surrounding development of online and distance education.

Both national and local governments are responsible for managing public and private primary and secondary education in Japan. The Ministry of Education, Culture, Sports, Science and Technology (MEXT) oversees infrastructure and policy by setting national curriculum standards, teacher certification programs, and requirements for setting up primary and secondary schools (National Center on Education and the Economy, 2016; OECD, 2015a). Local and municipal governments are both responsible for hiring teachers and managing budgets of public primary and secondary schools, and for providing partial funding to

private primary and secondary schools in the country. Compulsory education begins at first grade and ends at ninth grade; however, most Japanese children (95% of 4 years old, and 97% are 5 years old) are enrolled in *prepri-mary* education for the period before compulsory education begins (OECD, 2015a). Ninety-seven percent of all Japanese students also complete upper secondary school, and the majority (71%) are also expected to complete tertiary education (OECD, 2015a). Japan has also demonstrated excellent educational performance over the years in comparison to other countries. Japanese 15-year-olds, for example, ranked among the top five positions for science and mathematics, and the top ten positions for reading in the 2015 Program for International Student Assessment (PISA) exam (OECD, 2015b).

Because Japanese upper secondary schools are not compulsory, students must take entrance exams to attend upper secondary schools of their choice. These entrance exams are highly competitive because many individuals in Japan believe that studying at a better upper secondary school will lead to studying at a better university, consequently helping them obtain a better job in the future. To succeed in these secondary school entrance exams, many Japanese youth spend hours in private "cram" schools called *Juku* (塾、じゅく). Entrance exams are also required to enroll at most universities; therefore, many Japanese youth spend a significant amount of time and effort studying outside of their schools in private tutoring from the ages of 14 to 18.

Japanese tertiary education includes a diverse array of institutions. Japanese universities are similar to U.S. universities in that both offer bachelor degrees and graduate degrees in various academic disciplines. Unlike its U.S. counterparts, however, all Japanese universities, both public or private, are required to follow standards set by the Japanese government and are required to be regularly accredited by the government (Newby, Weko, Breneman, Johanneson, & Maassen, 2009). Junior colleges offer 2-year subdegree qualifications in liberal arts and vocational skills. Professional training colleges offer practical vocational and specialized technical education in various lengths, typically from 1-to-3 years of training. The most distinctive feature of Japanese tertiary education is that a high percentage of tertiary education institutions is private. Over 90% of junior colleges and professional training colleges are private institutions, as are nearly 78% of universities (Newby et al., 2009). The private educational organizational model results in an extremely high financial burden for students and their families. With the high cost of higher education and additional cost of private tutoring to prepare for entrance exams, low-income Japanese households are unlikely to be able to secure enrollment of tertiary education for their children (Newby et al., 2009). About 1 million post-high school students borrow money from government-sponsored loans, amounting to some 1.1 trillion yen (approximately U.S.$10 billion at the mid-2017 exchange rate) nationwide (Brasor & Tsubuku, 2016). By comparison, the U.S. has 77 million student borrowers holding some $1.3 trillion in debt (Center for Microeconomic Data, 2016, 2017).

Although the gender gap has narrowed in recent years, the gap still exists and requires improvement. Japan is one of only three OECD countries where more men attain tertiary education than women. A larger proportion of 25–34-year-old men (42%) compared to women (31%) had attained tertiary education by 2014 (OECD, 2015b). In addition to the gender gap in tertiary education participation, there is also a significant gender gap in employment participation. The rate of employment among Japanese women with tertiary degrees remains considerably lower than that of men (90% of men vs. 71% of women) (OECD, 2015b). Culturally, women are expected to take care of the majority of household chores and childrearing duties; therefore, a significant number of women leave their employment once their first child is born. Adult education participation may help women to return to the workforce, but Japan also has a wide gap in adult education participation. While 48% of men in Japan participated in adult education activities in 2012, only 35% of women did so in that same period, which is the largest gender gap in participation across OECD countries (OECD, 2017). A case can be made, then, that increased participation of women in tertiary and adult education could potentially contribute to Japan's future economic growth (OECD, 2014).

AN OVERVIEW OF DISTANCE EDUCATION IN JAPAN

Japan possesses a fairly long history of distance education. Historians generally agree that the origin of distance education in Japan can be traced back to "lecture notes" in the late 19th century (Aoki, 2011). Lecture notes were written by teachers to be used in class and published by universities during that period. These lecture notes were purchased as study materials both by students who were enrolled in schools and students who could not enroll in schools. Those who could not enroll in schools would study these lecture notes materials, then take exams to gain certification. In the 1940s, several higher education institutions established correspondence programs that were officially recognized by the government to offer bachelor's degree programs. These correspondence programs were created by established universities to provide access to their programs to those who otherwise could not attend traditional, face-to-face classes. The credits earned in these correspondence programs were recognized as equal in value to transcripts from traditional institutions. The government mandated that the degree-bearing correspondence programs offer 30 credit hours in face-to-face format per year. This annual mandate of 30 credit hours was later revised to allow the universities to offer this instruction via the Internet (Aoki, 2011). Currently, approximately 50 universities offer correspondence/distance education programs in Japan

(Ministry of Education, Culture, Sports, Science and Technology, 2016).

In addition to higher education distance education programs, Japan offers several other unique distance education programs. High school distance education programs were established in 1960s for those who could not attend regular high schools for economic or social reasons. In recent years, these high school programs have come to accommodate students with emotional challenges or mental illnesses, and allow them to continue education via the distance format. Additionally, correspondence/distance education is also a popular format in vocational and enrichment education fields. There are currently thousands of vocational and enrichment programs offered via correspondence or online formats. These program are popular among Japanese workers, students, and housewives because Japanese learners traditionally like to pursue many "shi-kaku" (資格、しかく)—official or unofficial vocational certificates—to expand their chances of getting a job as specialists in their fields of choice.

Distance Education
in Japanese Higher Education

In examining distance education in higher education in Japan, it is important to distinguish between distance education *programs* and distance education *courses*. Distance education programs are regulated differently from campus-based programs of higher education in Japan (Aoki, 2011). MEXT has created and maintained two separate accreditation standards: one for traditional on-campus institutions, and the other for correspondence education. Distance education programs are regulated under the standards of correspondence programs in Japan. Although on-campus and correspondence programs are accredited by different standards, credits earned on campus or correspondence programs are generally transferrable, particularly between specific institutions. In 2011, 44 universities provided undergraduate distance education programs,

and 217,236 students were seeking degrees at a distance, adding up to about 7.5% of total higher education enrollees (Aoki, 2012). The number of universities that offer distance education remains generally unchanged in recent years.

In addition to distance education programs, Japanese universities also offer individual distance education courses. According to 2016 data from MEXT, 64 (74%) of all national universities, 30 (34%) of all local public universities, and 168 (28%) of all private universities offer distance education courses in a variety of topics, spanning from remedial courses to credit-bearing professional courses. MEXT has published the number of distance education courses every year since 2006, but the number of universities that offer distance education courses has remained practically unchanged during the past 10 years.

One possible reason for this growth stagnation in Japanese distance education courses is due to the low adoption rate of learning management systems (LMS) in Japanese universities. According to a 2014 report from Kyoto University, 80% of universities have adopted an LMS on their campuses; however, only 1–20% of courses on these campuses are taught using their campus LMS (Kyoto University, 2014). Another possible reason is that many universities lack strategic visions and actual strategies for instructional technology and eLearning. Only 50% of universities have designated units for planning and implementing instructional technology on campus; moreover, in many universities, the work of incorporating technology in instruction is mostly organized around individual faculty members or groups of faculty members, rather than institutional initiatives (Kyoto University, 2014). The Kyoto University report also points out that 20–40% of universities do not have dedicated budgets or personnel for instructional technology, which plays into this dynamic.

Although the current state of distance education in Japan is a bit oblique, there nevertheless remain a few organizations that have made concerted efforts to develop online education.

In the following section, I discuss case studies of two such organizations: one, the Open University of Japan (OUJ), and two, the Japan Massive Open Online Education Promotion Council (JMOOC). I highlight the history, current efforts, and future directions of these organizations to discuss their contribution to the advancement of Japanese online education. In preparing this article, I interviewed representatives from both organizations and collected public data available from their organizational websites. Also integrated into this discussion is literature that sheds additional light on these organizations.

Open University of Japan

The OUJ has the distinction of being the only distance education university in Japan that broadcasts instructional programs over the public airwaves. OUJ was established by the Japanese government as a 4-year higher education institution in 1981. It started its television and radio broadcast instruction in April 1985, modeled somewhat after the British Open University (Aoki, 2012). Originally, the OUJ's principal methods of instruction included broadcast programs, printed text materials, and face-to-face schooling at 57 local study centers and support offices throughout Japan. In recent years, online classes have been added and students can take these online classes as a part of the face-to-face instruction requirement.

The OUJ requires all students to take at least 20 credit hours of the face-to-face instruction at the local study centers. Each face-to-face class is considered one credit and is taught over weekends. A total of 124 credit hours are required to graduate with a bachelor's degree, which is approximately equivalent to on-campus higher education in Japan. At least 94 of those credits must be completed via broadcasted courses, which are 15-weeks in length and offered once a week for 45 minutes each week. OUJ broadcasts these courses via TV, radio, and Internet. OUJ is not currently planning to replace TV and radio broadcasting with Internet broadcasting, as the government maintains the TV and radio modalities at OUJ to continue (S. Kisugi, personal communication, June 2, 2017). Each broadcast program enrolls more than 1,000 students.

OUJ is a relatively large higher education provider. The OUJ currently enrolls approximately 84,000 undergraduate students and 5,200 graduate students. About 45% of undergraduate students and 55% of graduate students are male; about 14% of undergraduates and 4% of graduate students are under 30 years old, while 45% of undergraduate and 59% of graduate are over the age of 50 (OUJ, 2017). About 10% of undergraduate and graduate students are retirees, which reflects the aging population of Japan. OUJ offers undergraduate degrees in liberal arts within five themed concentrations: *Human and Culture*, *Society and Industry* (including basic engineering*), Lifestyle and Welfare*, *Psychology and Education*, and *Nature and Environments* (including physics and chemistry). Approximately 340 subjects are offered by OUJ each year (OUJ, 2017).

In 2014, OUJ added online courses that could be used to meet the face-to-face instruction requirement mandated by Japanese government. OUJ currently offers 20 topics online and plans to increase towards 100 topics within a few years (S. Kisugi, personal communication, June 2, 2017). Online courses at OUJ employ the Moodle LMS, which provides students with video lectures, asynchronous discussion, assignments, and tests. Video lectures can be created fairly easily at OUJ because professors are very familiar with the broadcasting style of teaching, and production staff are available to assist them in their content development duties. In addition to video production staff, instructional designers, teaching assistants, and technical staff are available to assist teachers in creating online courses. Even with these additional support personnel, the president of OUJ stated during our interview that the instructor workload is an issue as they attempt to increase the number of online courses (S. Kisugi, personal communication, June 2, 2017). Moreover, humanities instructors tend to have stronger resistance to adopting online teaching although the reason for this is currently unknown (S. Kisugi, personal communication, June 2, 2017).

On the other hand, OUJ students typically have little resistance to taking online courses and actually enjoy online courses. One reason for student preference for online courses is the frequency of assessments: students in online courses are not required to take final exams due to frequent assessments during the semester, but for all broadcast and face-to-face courses, final exams are required and administered at one of their local study centers (S. Kisugi, personal communication, June 2, 2017).

OUJ will be facing some interesting opportunities and challenges in the near future. OUJ's funding is currently 56% from government sources and 41% from student tuition. This funding structure is a "double-edged sword," because on one hand government funding allows OUJ to maintain low tuition and thus stay comparably affordable within the higher education market. On the other hand, the government's specific requirements in OUJ's operation strongly influences the future direction of the institution. The President of OUJ, Shin Kisugi (S. Kisugi, personal communication, June 2, 2017), described two primary methods which the government employs to determine OUJ's future direction. The first approach, which concerns program offerings, is the government's request that certain areas of studies should be offered at the university. It is challenging for the university to respond to this request because OUJ has traditionally offered liberal arts education, and program offering requests places an additional financial burden upon the institution. Second, OUJ is concerned that the institution may lose government funding if OUJ attempts to transition some of their broadcast courses to the online environment because OUJ was originally established to offer broadcast courses. Despite these challenges, OUJ intends to expand their certificate programs. Currently, OUJ offers

approximately 20 certificates, including qualifications to take national certification exams for education, nursing, accounting, social work and psychology.

The Japanese government's regulations on OUJ to offer broadcast courses could also have a strong impact on the pedagogy of OUJ's educational offerings (Aoki, 2012). Aoki posits that teaching on broadcast media molds OUJ's teaching approach to a cognitive-behavioral approach, where students passively receive information from instructors, and limits OUJ's freedom to advance teaching to social-constructivist or constructivist approaches, where students actively interact with instructors and peers to construct new knowledge and ideas. Aoki (2012) argues that OUJ must reorganize its structure and work with the government to relax regulations, permitting new styles of teaching and learning that place students at the center of learning and accommodate the needs of diverse learners in the Japanese environment.

Japan Massive Open Online Education Promotion Council (JMOOC)

In an effort to globalize their *OpenCourse-Ware* initiative, the Massachusetts Institute of Technology (MIT) in the early 2000s approached several prestigious Japanese universities to offer information technology course content as a part of that initiative. In 2005, a group of Japanese universities launched the *Japan OpenCourseWare Consortium* (JOCW), and the member organizations began preparation for open courseware (OCW) sites. Because the program is not designed to offer content as online courses (because these courses do not offer learning activities or assessments that students could currently complete and receive feedback via an online modality), some JOCW member universities subsequently decided to create a new MOOC to offer interactive online courses, thereby establishing the *Japan Massive Online Open Education Promotion Council (JMOOC)* in

November of 2013. These MOOC-based courses were first offered in April 2014.

Although JMOOC started as a consortium of universities, the initiative now also includes corporate and individual members. Unlike MOOCs in the United States, JMOOC is a member-driven organization and fully funded by membership dues (Y. Fukuhara, personal communication, May 10, 2017). Annual membership dues structure includes premium corporate members who pay 5,000,000 yen (approximately U.S.$45,000 at the mid-2017 exchange rate), regular corporate members that pay 500,000 yen or more (about U.S.$4,500+), other nonprofit members that pay 100,000 yen or more (U.S.$900), and individual members that pay 10,000 yen (U.S.$90). Currently, JMOOC has six premium members (all business institutions), 89 regular members (49 universities, 32 business institutions, and eight miscellaneous organizations) and nine nonprofit members. Fukuhara (2017) stated that this funding structure is considered more sustainable than the American model, where only a few organizations or corporations fund the operation of any particular MOOC. In addition to the memberships, three corporations and one university are providing "in-kind" service by hosting and operating MOOC platforms for JMOOC (Y. Fukuhara, personal communication, May 10, 2017).

As of 2017, JMOOC offers 181 courses on a wide variety of topics including business management, humanities, social sciences, computer programming, education, natural science, statistics, mathematics, arts, and engineering. Course offerings are determined by individual member universities, corporations, and organizations. JMOOC is planning to continue these types of course offerings; however, JMOOC is also making a concerted effort to offer courses that Japanese industry and businesses need to maintain competitive advantage in an increasingly global business world (Y. Fukuhara, personal cCommunication, May 10, 2017).

In response to a federal policy on human resource development in science and engineering in 2016, the Japan Business Federation (a federation of 1,500+ member organizations in business and industry), as well as representatives from higher education, met to discuss the challenges of providing recent college graduates with practical technical foundation skills that prepares them for advanced technical jobs. The Japan Business Federation sent a survey to early career engineers asking what training has helped engineers for the first few years of their work in business. More than 400 engineers from nine Japan Business Federation member corporations responded to the survey. Based on the results of the survey and with the consultation with the Japan Business Federation, JMOOC developed a series of practical foundational technical skill courses for IT engineers that help them transition to corporate environments. This series consists of 12 courses, including courses in programming, artificial intelligence, applied software design, project management, and networking. JMOOC started the series for IT engineers in the spring of 2017 and hopes to create an additional five series of some 60 courses for engineers employed within industrial technology, chemical engineering, mechanical engineering, and civil engineering jobs. JMOOC expects that their corporate members and clients will use these courses as a part of new employee training, or for professional development training for existing employees. JMOOC is also desirous that their university members will use these courses as a part of "flipped classrooms" within their university face-to-face classes (Y. Fukuhara, personal communication, May 10, 2017). JMOOC is thus uniquely situated and well-integrated into the fabric of Japanese economic development and government-industry-education collaboration

JMOOC had 380,000 unique users in 2015 (Fukuhara, 2017). Sixty-seven percent of those enrolled were male, 61% held full-time employment while studying, and 63% were college graduates. The age of participants consisted of 20% each for ages of 20s, 30s, 40s, and 50s; the remaining 20% were either teens or older than 60. The majority of JMOOC participants were of working age (Fukuhara, 2017). Thus, JMOOC appears to cater toward individuals with secure employment who are looking to improve their careers or to satisfy their professional and personal interests. The JMOOC current completion rate is 15%, which is higher than that of other U.S.-based MOOCs, which hovers around 6.5% (Jordan, 2014). The completion rate is even higher for technically advanced JMOOC courses (Y. Fukuhara, personal communication, May 10, 2017).

JMOOC science and engineering courses are 6 to 8 weeks long; other courses are 4 weeks in length. Each week consists of 5 to 10 lessons that include two sets of a 10-minute lecture video and an accompanying quiz, discussion board, and a peer-reviewed assignment. Each course also includes a cumulative course assignment. The courses are designed to allow busy employees to take lessons they need from a course as well as to take entire courses while they continue their employment. A unique feature of JMOOC courses is that participants can enter a unique company ID to directly send academic progress to their companies (Y. Fukuhara, personal communication, May 10, 2017). This feature is part of corporate membership benefit, which costs U.S.$4,500 annually. Approximately 30% of JMOOC courses offer the optional flipped classes, where students can pay an additional fee (3,500–5,000 yen, or about U.S.$32–45) to attend face-to-face classroom sessions that can promote their learning in MOOC courses.

With these unique membership and instructional features, and with effective government-industry collaboration, JMOOC has all the hallmarks of success in online education. However, JMOOC's Fukuhara (personal communication, May 10, 2017) notes several challenges. First, despite JMOOC's intentions to increase the number of course offerings, particularly in science and engineering, member universities often lack the infrastructure required to create a MOOC course. Support staff, such as instructional designers and media specialists, are not common in Japan; thus, universities that desire to create a MOOC course may need to out-

source such support staff. As mentioned previously in this article, many Japanese universities also lack dedicated budgets or offices for instructional technology; therefore, individual faculty members must each locate budget and personnel that can help them develop and teach a MOOC course. Additionally, faculty support is not commonplace in many universities; therefore, faculty members may not know how to effectively teach in an online environment. For example, JMOOC currently does not offer faculty training to those who would like to teach in their system.

The second challenge JMOOC faces is related to their enrollment and client base. According to a research conducted by JMOOC and NTT Communication Online Marketing Research, Inc., 78% of respondents generally did not know about MOOCs (JMOOC & NTT Communication Online Marketing Research, 2016). Approximately half of respondents expressed interest in participating in MOOCs in the future. The most cited reasons for *not* wanting to participate are lack of time, interest, and motivation (JMOOC & NTT Communication Online Marketing Research, 2016). Thus, it is crucial for JMOOC to increase awareness of MOOCs among Japanese population in general and offer practical and engaging courses to attract more participants.

Additionally, JMOOC faces a challenge in increasing the number and types of courses that will attract additional participants. As discussed earlier, JMOOC already has a strategy to increase engineering and science course offerings in response to industry needs and governmental initiatives to develop human resources in these fields. In addition to science and engineering courses, JMOOC is planning to increase the number of courses in business-related topics, including finance, marketing, and accounting. JMOOC is additionally planning to increase course offerings that prepare individuals to become global citizens. JMOOC believes that global citizens require not only English skills, but also a foundational knowledge of liberal arts, history, and philosophy in order to communicate with people from different countries and cultures. Such courses would attract more enrollment among their current customer base (i.e., 20s–50s working adults), but would also attract mature audiences, such as retirees and workers approaching retirement as they look for courses in personal enrichment.

JMOOC's short-range goals are to increase the number of offered courses to 100+, university members to over 100 institutions, and enrollment to 1,000,000 students in the next few years (Fukuhara, 2017). Despite these ambitious goals, JMOOC may face a challenge in attracting technologically savvy university members due to the lack of infrastructure and budget within Japanese universities. One of the incentives for universities to join JMOOC is that JMOOC courses can be used to showcase their faculty's teaching and to attract students from other countries (personal communication, May 10, 2017). All JMOOC courses are captioned in Japanese; this technique could aid foreign students in understanding course content and preparing them to participate classes when they are matriculated to study in Japan. Moreover, JMOOC would need to explore additional creative approaches to gain participation from higher education institutions and their faculty. It is also crucial to address the issue of the burden placed upon on faculty when creating a MOOC course. Therefore, it may be advisable for JMOOC to assist member universities by staffing instructional designers to streamline course design and planning, media specialists to work on video production, and faculty developers who can work with faculty to teach more effectively in an online environment.

SUGGESTIONS AND RECOMMENDATIONS FOR UNIVERSITIES IN EXPANDING ONLINE EDUCATION

The Overall Popularity of Online Education in Japan

As of 2017, Japanese online education has but a few key players such as OUJ and JMOOC that have found their own unique niches, employed continuous strategic efforts, and gained support from the government and industry. In addition to these two organizations, approximately 40 other universities offer distance education programs that grant undergraduate degrees to students who cannot attend on-campus programs. Although these programs are available, online education remains generally unpopular in Japanese higher education. One of the fundamental challenges for Japanese universities is that these institutions usually do not attract nontraditional students. According to the most recent OECD data, participation in formal education by 25–64-year-olds in Japan is 2.4%, and much lower than the OECD average of 10% (OECD, 2016). Participation in both formal and nonformal education by 25–64-year-olds in Japan is 40%, compared to OECD average of 50%; thus, formal education institutions, including universities, are not a place of choice for 25-year or older students to further their educational goals or gain new qualifications. Considering that lack of time, interest, and motivation are cited as reasons for nonparticipation in MOOCs (JMOOC & NTT Communication Online Marketing Research, 2016), Japanese universities need to come up with flexible course formats and practical course offerings for those who may want to complete college degrees later in their lives.

The low rate of participation in formal education also stems from Japanese business practice that favors traditional-aged college graduates without job experience rather than nontraditional-aged college students with working experience. With a recent low birth rate and a projected shortage of working-age adults in the near future, this practice may be forced to change. Therefore, online Japanese universities may be well positioned to train those who would like to obtain college degrees and advance their careers later in life. A university named "Cyber University," for example, is already targeting nontraditional-aged students in Japan. Three-quarters of Cyber University students are older than 25

(Kawahara, 2016). Online education is suitable for working adults because it offers flexible scheduling and locations, and an inclusive environment where students with different background (i.e., older students and those with mobility issues or social difficulty) may not visibly stand out from traditional-aged college students.

Online Education and Women

In addition to catering to adult learners, online education may also become a great vehicle for women who hope to reenter the workforce after their children are grown. As discussed earlier, participation of women in the workforce, in tertiary education, and in adult education are all low in Japan, and women are severely underutilized in the society (OECD, 2014, 2015b). A low birth rate and a shrinking workforce also may require a shift in the culture and create an environment where women can thrive within the workforce. Flexible scheduling and inclusive environment with no visible differences in online education should be theoretically optimal for housewives who may not have time to participate in on-campus programs, or may feel excluded from traditional-aged university students. Therefore, it is critical that online education create a welcoming environment for people with diverse backgrounds and offer additional services (such as training on using computers, writing reports, and using quantitative skills) that help students to transition into higher education.

Recommendations for Structural and Pedagogical Changes

In order to expand online education, Japanese universities should invest in a variety of structural and pedagogical changes. As for structural changes, institutions need to create an infrastructure that permits their faculty to employ instructional technology more easily than currently is the case. As discussed earlier, Japanese universities have a low rate of LMS

adoption, and even the institutions that *have* adopted LMS rely heavily on faculty, not technology support staff, to plan, implement, and integrate instructional technology into teaching (Kyoto University, 2014). Most recent data show that only 40% of universities keep track of the number of courses conducted using an LMS (Academic eXchange for Information Environment and Strategy, 2015), which illustrates that LMS adoption is extremely decentralized in Japanese universities. In addition to LMS adoption, only 50% of universities have designated units for planning and implementing instructional technology on campus (Kyoto University, 2014). If Japanese universities wish to attract students with different backgrounds to online education, these universities will be required to allocate sufficient resources and to create dedicated units to plan and implement instructional technology.

In addition to the infrastructure, hiring experienced instructional technology support staff is crucial for the success of online education. Instructional designers and media specialists can help ease a faculty's workload in creating online courses. The preference of video-based, teacher-centered online courses in Japan (Funamori, 2015) makes creating courses time consuming. If text-based, student centered online courses similar to the ones in U.S. higher education were adopted in Japan, faculty workload could be reduced. Although it may be ideal to encourage Japanese universities to alter their pedagogical approaches to a more student-centered approach, this change would require a fundamental shift within the culture of Japanese higher education. Therefore, in the short-term, it may be desirable to offer Japanese students the familiar video-based, teacher-centered, lecture format online courses. Instructional designers who understand the unique cultural constraints associated with this environment would therefore be valuable to universities that would like to expand online education. Suzuki (2009) notes that "e-Learning Consortium Japan" offers an online master's program for e-learning specialists. Recruiting qualified instructional designers, particularly those sensitive to the cultures present in the Japanese context, could be beneficial to online learning at universities in Japan.

Japanese universities could also undertake pedagogical transformations to expand online education offerings. As Aoki (2012) points out, online education programs in Japan are still using cognitive-behavioral pedagogies, where students receive knowledge in a one-way direction from faculty to learner, and where student-faculty/peer interactions are rare. Aoki (2012) posits that this type of pedagogy is making it difficult for Japanese universities to teach within the online environment. According to the 2007 National College Student Survey (University of Tokyo, 2007), 82% of courses are taught in the traditional lecture format, only approximately 30% of courses solicit student's opinions in class, and only 37% of courses have activities that require active student participation. Thus, Japanese universities heavily employ a teacher-centered knowledge-transfer style of teaching. Although a 2009 Central Council of Education Report emphasizes problem-solving, analytical, and communication skills as important goals for Japanese higher education (Japanese Central Council of Education, 2009), those skills are almost impossible to develop in students without adopting teaching methods that employ student-centered teaching and active learning. Therefore, it is critical that faculty receive training in active learning strategies and student-centered pedagogy. Faculty development activities at Japanese universities have been mandated by MEXT since 2008. Although the faculty development activities at the university level are mandated by the government, the specific types of activities or participation of individual faculty members are not (Suzuki, 2013). Thus, in order to promote participation in professional development activities, higher education institutions should create a culture where teaching is evaluated as part of their faculty promotion processes, as well as provide faculty incentives to take advantage of faculty development opportunities.

CONCLUSION

Although Japan is famous for its level of technological advancement, the development of online education programs has lagged due to various cultural challenges surrounding both the existing educational and employment cultural contexts. Life-long learning, especially at formal education institutions such as universities and colleges, is not common; therefore, only a small number of formal education institutions have implemented online degree programs. Hiring practices in Japan that show a strong preference for hiring new graduates of traditional college age contribute to a lack of learner interest in formal life-long education. In terms of online courses offered through brick-and-mortar universities, development has also been slow because about only half of Japanese universities have dedicated units and budgets for implementing and maintaining instructional technology. Thus, cultural and structural changes are crucial if Japan is serious about fuller adoption and integration of online education.

Despite these limitations, two institutions have found niches in online and distance education, and have a promising outlook. The OUJ has been partially funded by the Japanese government to offer undergraduate and graduate degrees to students throughout Japan. Although their chief method of instruction is still broadcast media, OUJ has begun offering online courses that have been well received by students. Some faculty members resist the move toward online education; however, it would be relatively easy for OUJ to move their lectures into an online environment because OUJ's teaching staff is used to delivering lectures to students at distance. In the future, OUJ may also face challenges from governmental restrictions as they attempt to expand their online education.

The JMOOC, on the other hand, is a membership-driven organization that has a strong relationship with the Japanese government, business, and industrial sectors. JMOOC, funded mainly by business and university members, has developed its expansion plans by incorporating input from the Japan Business Federation, and will expand its offerings in science, engineering and business that can be used as part of professional development training for member corporations, or as part of college classes at member universities.

In order to create a more effective online learning environment, all Japanese higher education institutions could benefit from implementation of a pedagogical shift that supports online learning. The current teacher-centered "knowledge transfer" model of teaching, evidenced in a large section of the higher education system, is simply insufficient to prepare students with problem-solving, analytical, and communication skills. Thus, it is important for Japanese university faculty to learn student-centered active learning methods of teaching in *both* face-to-face and online environments, and for Japanese universities to provide faculty support and create a culture that encourages student-centered learning.

At the national level, it is important to focus on women, as well as nontraditional-aged students because these populations can become great contributors to the future of the Japanese economy, particularly as the workforce continues to shrink and the population continues to age. Online education can be a great vehicle to encourage women and nontraditional-aged students to acquire additional education to prepare for future workforce because they may feel more integrated into their classrooms in an online environment where their identity may not stand out as greatly as in face-to-face environment. Collaboration among government, industry, and higher education is essential to allow these untapped talents to be developed and integrated into the future workforce in Japan.

This article has discussed and provided evidence that online education needs to play a greater role within the Japanese higher education system. Whether such a transformation will occur, and to what extent it might, remains an open question as the Japanese higher educational system and the Japanese government assesses its options for 21st century education.

REFERENCES

Academic eXchange for Information Environment and Strategy. (2015). 2015 Chousa *Koutou kyouikukikantou ni okeru ICT no rikatuyou ni kansuru chousakenkyu* [2015 Survey: Research on utilization of ICT in higher education institutions etc.]. Retrieved from https://axies.jp/ja/ict/2015

Aoki, K. (2011). The challenges of ICT applications in distance higher education in Japan, *Distances et saviors, 9,* 27–40.

Aoki, K. (2012). Generations of distance education and challenges of distance education Institutions in Japanese Higher Education. In P. B. Muyinda (Ed.), *Distance Education, InTech.* Retrieved from https://www.intechopen.com/books/distance-education/generations-of-distance-education-and-challenges-of-distance-education-institutions-in-japanese-high

Brasor, P., & Tubuku, M. (2016, January 23). Mounting student debt may cost society dearly. *The Japan Times.* Retrieved from https://www.japantimes.co.jp/news/2016/01/23/business/mounting-student-debt-may-cost-society-dearly/#.WcE_A9Frzcs

Center for Microeconomic Data. (2016). *2016 student loan data update* [Data file]. Retrieved from https://www.newyorkfed.org/medialibrary/interactives/householdcredit/data/xls/sl_update_2016.xlsx

Center for Microeconomic Data. (2017). *Quarterly report on household debt and credit* [Data file]. Retrieved from https://www.newyorkfed.org/medialibrary/interactives/householdcredit/data/xls/HHD_C_Report_2017Q2.xlsx

Central Intelligent Agency. (2017). *The world factbook: Japan.* Retrieved from https://www.cia.gov/library/publications/the-world-factbook/geos/ja.html

Crawford, R. J. (1998). Reinterpreting the Japanese economic miracle. *Harvard Business Review, 76,* 178–183.

Fukuhara, Y. (2017). *Kaigai MOOC no doukou to JMOOC no genjou* [Current situations of MOOC abroad and JMOOC]. [PowerPoint] JMOOC, Tokyo, Japan.

Funamori, M. (2015). *Sekai youryoku daigaku online kyouiku consortium ga kouotoukyouikuni ataeru eikyou no kenkyu* [The impact of MOOCs on higher education]. Retrieved from https://kaken.nii.ac.jp/ja/file/KAKENHI-PROJECT-25590219/25590219seika.pdf

Green, F., & Henseke G. (2016). Should governments of OECD countries worry about graduate underemployment? *Oxford Review of Economic Policy, 32*, 514–537.

JMOOC & NTT Communication Online Marketing Research. (2016). *Daigaku no opunka ni kansuru chousakekka* [Survey result of university openness]. Retrieved from http://research.nttcoms.com/database/data/002043/

The Japanese Central Council of Education. (2009). *Gakushikateikyouiku no kouchikunimukete.* [Towards building of undergraduate education]. Retrieved from http://www.mext.go.jp/component/b_menu/shingi/toushin/__icsFiles/afieldfile/2008/12/26/1217067_001.pdf

Jordan, K. (2014). Initial trends in enrolment and completion of massive open online courses. *The International Review of Research in Open and Distributed Learning, 15*, 133–160.

Kawahara, H. (2016). *Shougaigakushu nizu heno online kyouiku no kouka* [Effectiveness of online education in response to lifelong learning]. Retrieved from http://www.cyber-u.ac.jp/about/pdf/e-learning/0005/CU_e005_01.pdf

Kyoto University. (2014). *Koutou kyouikukikantou ni okeru ICT no rikatuyou ni kansuru chousakenkyu* [Research on utilization of ICT in higher education institutions, etc.]. Retrieved from http://www.mext.go.jp/a_menu/koutou/itaku/1347642.htm

The Ministry of Education, Culture, Sports, Science and Technology. (2016) *Monbukagaku Tokei Yoran* [Mext Statistics Summary]. Retrieved from http://www.mext.go.jp/component/b_menu/other/__icsFiles/afieldfile/2016/06/02/1368897_10.xls

National Center on Education and the Economy. (2016). *Japan: System and school organization.* Retrieved from http://ncee.org/what-we-do/center-on-international-education-benchmarking/top-performing-countries/japan-overview/japan-system-and-school-organization/

Newby, H., Weko, T., Breneman, D., Johanneson, T., & Maassen, P. (2009). *OECD review of tertiary education: Japan.* Retrieved from https://www.oecd.org/japan/42280329.pdf

Organization for Economic Co-operation and Development. (2014). *Education at glance: Country notes—Japan.* Retrieved from http://www.oecd.org/edu/Japan-EAG2014-Country-Note.pdf

Organization for Economic Co-operation and Development. (2015a). *Education policy outlook: Japan.* Retrieved from https://www.oecd.org/edu/Japan-country-profile.pdf

Organization for Economic Co-operation and Development. (2015b). *PISA 2015 Results.* Retrieved from http://www.keepeek.com/Digital-Asset-Management/oecd/education/pisa-2015-results-volume-i_9789264266490-en#.WY3CEemQzct

Organization for Economic Co-operation and Development. (2016). *Education at glance.* Retrieved from http://www.oecd.org/edu/education-at-a-glance-19991487.htm

Organization for Economic Co-operation and Development. (2017). *Adult education and learning.* Retrieved from https://stats.oecd.org/Index.aspx?DataSetCode=EAG_AL

Open University of Japan. (2017). *Suji de miru OUJ* [OUJ data overview]. Retrieved from http://www.ouj.ac.jp/hp/gaiyo/number/

Suzuki, K. (2009). From competency list to curriculum implementation: A case study of Japan's first online master's program for e-learning specialists training. *International Journal on E-Learning, 8,* 469–478.

University of Tokyo. (2007) *Zenkoku daigakusei chousa* [National survey of university students]. Retrieved from http://ump.p.u-tokyo.ac.jp/crump/resource/kiso2008_01.pdf

World Bank. (2017). *Gross domestic product 2016.* Retrieved from http://databank.worldbank.org/data/download/GDP.pdf

CONFERENCE CALENDAR

Charles Schlosser
Nova Southeastern University

The following conferences may be of interest to the readers of the *Quarterly Review of Distance Education.*

ISTE, June 24-27, Chicago, IL

"The ISTE Conference & Expo is recognized globally as the most comprehensive educational technology conference in the world. For more than three decades, educators and education leaders have gathered at the ISTE conference to engage in hands-on learning, exchange ideas and network with like-minded thinkers seeking to transform learning and teaching. The annual event attracts over 16,000 attendees and industry representatives, including teachers, technology coordinators, administrators, library media specialists, teacher educators and policymakers. Attendees also enjoy world-class keynotes, hundreds of sessions in a variety of formats and a massive expo hall."
https://conference.iste.org/2018/

EdMedia, June 25-29, Amsterdam, The Netherlands

"EdMedia + Innovate Learning, the premier international conference in the field since 1987, spans all disciplines and levels of education attracting researchers and practitioners in the field from 70+ countries. This annual conference offers a forum for the discussion and exchange of research, development, and applications on all topics related to Innovation and Education."
https://www.aace.org/conf/edmedia/

Distance Teaching & Learning Conference, August 7–9, Madison, WI

"DT&L isn't just a conference, it's a community of educators with ideas and experiences to share. You'll laugh, you'll be moved, and you'll come away with new ways to approach your work and put research into practice. You'll meet people who can help your career thrive. You'll also get to enjoy Madison—a walkable, culture-filled city nestled between two beautiful lakes. It's the perfect place to learn, explore, and relax this summer."
https://dtlconference.wisc.edu/

E-Learn World Conference on E-Learning, October 15–18, Las Vegas, NV

"E-Learn World Conference on E-Learning is an international conference organized by the

• **Charles Schlosser**, Associate Professor Emeritus, Fischler College of Education, Nova Southeastern University, 3301 College Avenue, Fort Lauderdale, FL 33314. E-mail: charles.schlosser@nova.edu

The Quarterly Review of Distance Education, Volume 18(3), 2017, pp. 89–90   ISSN 1528-3518

AACE-Association for the Advancement of Computing in Education and cosponsored by the *International Journal on E-Learning*. E-Learn provides a unique forum for government, healthcare, education, and business professionals to discuss the latest research, development, applications, issues, and strategies, to explore new technologies, and to identify solutions for today's challenges related to online learning. A variety of opportunities and venues are designed to enable participants to actively learn from and collaborate with a multinational, cross-industry expert faculty and peers on the research, development, diverse learning experiences, implementation and technology needed to improve e-learning."
https://www.aace.org/conf/elearn/

AECT International Convention, October 23–27, Kansas City, MO

"The AECT International Convention brings together participants from around the world, offering practical applications, cutting-edge research, hands-on workshops, and demonstrations of new technologies in teaching and learning. Take this opportunity to connect with your peers! The goal of the convention is for participants from around the world to learn from the experiences and activities of the convention, enriching their professional lives."
http://members.aect.org/events/call/

AUTHOR BIOGRAPHICAL DATA

Kathlyn Bradshaw is a professor in the School of Business at Algonquin College School of Business. Her area of specialization is business communications. In addition, she teaches online for Oxford University. Bradshaw's current research interests open educational resources (OER), specifically cultural historical activity theory and massive open online course (MOOC) design.

Victoria Ingalls is an associate professor of mathematics at Tiffin University. Upon completion of her undergraduate degree in mathematics education at Bowling Green State University, Ingalls began teaching at a local high school while earning her master's of education degree from Heidelberg College. She launched her collegiate career by lecturing as an adjunct instructor at a variety of local colleges and began teaching full-time at Tiffin University in the mathematics department in 2007. Ingalls completed her doctoral education from Ashland University in 2008. She lives in Tiffin with her husband and five daughters.

Jennifer Lock is a Professor and the Associate Dean of Teaching and Learning in the Werklund School of Education at the University of Calgary. Her area of specialization is the learning sciences. Lock's current research interests are in e-learning, change and innovation in education, scholarship of teaching and learning in higher education, and makerspaces.

Christopher Masullo is a technology coordinator and facilitator. His credentials include being certified as a principal and supervisor as well as a school administrator. He earned a doctorate in instructional technology and distance education and a master's degree in educational administration and supervision. He has served as chairperson of the Mathematics and Technology Curriculum Committee; served as the resource person for all teaching staff regarding the effective integration of technology into the teaching-learning process; implemented and directed STEM initiatives; managed summer enrichment programs; and conducted professional development workshops for staff members.

Kelly McKenna is an assistant professor in the Adult Education and Training Program in the School of Education at Colorado State University. Her research interests lie in the field of adult education, with research objectives aimed to support adult learners in their educational and occupational endeavors by creating optimal learning environments and facilitating successful student experiences. She focuses on distance education, technology-enhanced teaching and learning, and learning communities.

Mayuko Nakamura is a faculty development coordinator and an adjunct instructor of Psychology at Illinois State University. She earned her master's degree from Teachers College, Columbia University in 1997 and has

The Quarterly Review of Distance Education, Volume 18(3), 2017, pp. 91–92   ISSN 1528-3518
Copyright © 2017 Information Age Publishing, Inc.   All rights of reproduction in any form reserved.

been working in higher education for the past 20 years.

Anymir Orellana is an associate professor in the Abraham S. Fischler College of Education, Nova Southeastern University (NSU). She earned a doctor of education in instructional technology and distance education from NSU; a master of science in computer and information sciences and engineering from the University of Florida; and a bachelor of science in informatics engineering from Universidad Centroccidental "Lisandro Alvarado" (UCLA), Venezuela. Since 2006 she has taught online doctoral courses in Spanish and English at NSU, in her areas of interest such as instructional media; instructional technology; distance education; curriculum, teaching, and technology; system analysis and design; and instructional design. She serves as applied dissertation chair and committee member to doctoral students. From 1997 to 2005 she was a professor at UCLA in the areas of computer data structures and analysis of computer algorithms in the in the BS in informatics engineering, and in the MS in information systems.

Gale Parchoma is an associate professor in the Department of Curriculum Studies in the College of Education at the University of Saskatchewan, and the coordinator of Canada's Collaboration for Online Higher Education Research. Her current research interests are in design thinking, simulation-based education, distributed cognition, and sociomateriality.

Donna Rennar-Potacco is the founder and director of a science resource center and an adjunct professor in the College of Science and Health at William Paterson University (WPUNJ) in the departments of Biology and Mathematics. She earned a doctor of education in instructional technology and distance education from Nova Southeastern University, a master of science in biochemistry and bachelor of science degree in chemistry from Rutgers University, and a master of business administration from Fairleigh Dickinson University. Previously, Rennar-Potacco worked in several university research laboratories and held a variety of corporate management positions that included laboratory development and systems auditing. She has authored numerous scholarly publications and presentations in the areas of student support, online learning, technology, academic support, and management.

Andres Salazar received an MS degree in scientific computing from New York University's Courant Institute. He is currently working as a quantitative marketing analyst for IDT Telecom, a global telecommunications operator with over $1.4 billion in revenue. Andres' expertise in data science and statistical methods has helped IDT to allocate off-line marketing spending more efficiently. At IDT, he helps to develop strategies and CRM campaigns based on customer purchasing behaviors. He is also an adjunct lecturer for the Baruch College–City University of New York.

CPSIA information can be obtained
at www.ICGtesting.com
Printed in the USA
FFOW01n1437180618
47172019-49818FF

9 781641 1320